Preface

As we move deeper into the 21st century, the role of technology in our lives continues to expand at an unprecedented pace. Among the most transformative technologies of our time is Artificial Intelligence (AI), which is increasingly becoming a cornerstone of innovation in virtually every field. From healthcare and education to entertainment and transportation, AI shapes how we live, work, and interact with the world around us. For today's students, understanding AI is not just an option—it's a necessity. This textbook, meticulously crafted for Class 7 students under the CBSE curriculum, is an essential guide to navigating the fascinating and rapidly evolving world of Artificial Intelligence.

The primary goal of this book is to understand AI, making it accessible and engaging for young learners. With its technical jargon and complex algorithms, AI can often seem intimidating. However, through this textbook, we have endeavoured to present AI in a clear, relatable, and intriguing. Each chapter is carefully designed to introduce fundamental concepts and principles of AI, ensuring that students not only understand the theoretical aspects but also see the practical relevance of AI in their everyday lives. Whether it's exploring how AI helps power their favourite apps, understanding how it assists doctors in diagnosing diseases, or learning how it's used to improve transportation systems, students will see first-hand how AI is woven into the fabric of modern society.

We have incorporated various interactive elements throughout the book to make the learning experience more engaging and effective. These include hands-on activities, project-based learning opportunities, and thought-provoking exercises that encourage students to apply what they've learned creatively and innovatively. By working through these activities, students will deepen their understanding of AI and develop critical thinking, problem-solving, and analytical skills that are vital in the digital age.

This textbook is more than just an introduction to AI—it's a call to action. It invites students to be curious, experiment, ask questions, and explore AI's vast possibilities. By nurturing curiosity and creativity from a young age, we can empower students to become tomorrow's innovators, thinkers, and leaders. The journey into the world of AI is just beginning, and this book is your companion on that journey, guiding you as you discover, learn, and grow.

As you embark on this exciting adventure into Artificial Intelligence, we encourage you to approach each chapter with an open mind and a spirit of exploration. Today's learners are shaping the future, and we are excited to see the incredible things you will achieve as you dive into the world of AI. Remember, the knowledge you gain today is the foundation for the innovations of tomorrow.

Table of Contents

Chapter 1: Advanced Concepts in Artificial Intelligence

Learning Objectives

History and Evolution of AI
Types of AI: Narrow, General, and Super AI
Role of Algorithms in AI
How AI Processes Data and Learns
Types of AI Algorithms
Importance of Feedback in AI

1.1 Recap of AI concepts

1.1.1 What is AI?

AI, or Artificial Intelligence, refers to the ability of machines, especially computers, to mimic or replicate intelligent human behaviour. AI is a super-smart assistant that learns from experience, solves problems, and makes data-driven decisions. Unlike traditional software, which follows predefined instructions, AI can improve its performance over time by analysing new information.

Example: Imagine you ask Google Assistant to set a reminder or play your favourite song. When you say, "Hey Google, remind me to call mother at 5 PM," AI processes your request, understands the task, and sets the reminder for you. Similarly, when you ask it to play a song, AI scans through its Database, finds the song, and plays it instantly. The system is not just following a fixed script; it understands and responds to your commands.

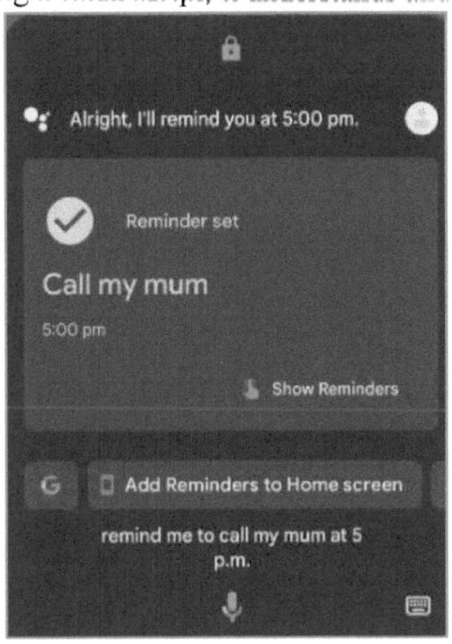

Fun Fact: The first AI program was created in 1951 and designed to play checkers. The program could learn from its mistakes and improve over time, much like modern AI systems that learn from the Data they are fed.

Artificial Intelligence vs. Human Intelligence: AI is powerful and efficient in performing specific tasks, such as analysing large Datasets or recognising patterns, but it's different from Human Intelligence. AI doesn't have feelings, emotions, or consciousness. While AI can learn from Data, it cannot think creatively, understand context beyond its programming, or experience the world like a human does.

1.1.2 Computer Vision

This field of AI enables machines to interpret visual Data from the world around them. AI systems can analyse and make sense of images and videos, enabling tasks like Facial Recognition or Object Detection.

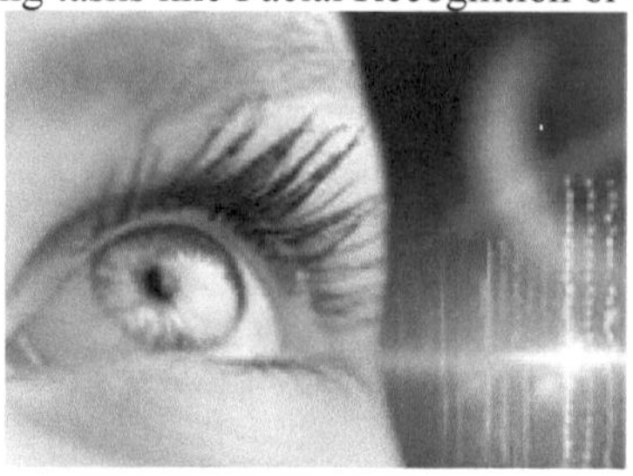

Comparison Activity: Ask students to list daily activities, such as brushing their teeth, deciding what to eat, or playing a game. Then, discuss whether AI could perform these tasks and compare how well AI might do to humans. For example, could AI choose a healthy breakfast or play a video game as skilfully as a person? This activity helps students understand the current limitations of AI.

1.1.3 Computing Power: The Engine behind AI

Computing Power refers to the speed and capacity of computers to process Data and run algorithms. The stronger the computing power, the more Data the AI can handle and the faster it can work. High-performance computers are crucial for AI to perform complex tasks, such as analysing thousands of medical images in seconds or translating languages in real-time.

For AI to recognise faces in photos, large amounts of image Data must be processed quickly. This requires powerful computers to analyse multiple images simultaneously and compare them to millions of stored images to find a match.

Fun Fact: The world's fastest supercomputer, Fugaku, located in Japan, can perform over 442 quadrillion calculations per second! To visualise this, imagine every person on Earth doing 55 million calculations simultaneously!

1.2 History and Evolution of AI

The History of Artificial Intelligence is marked by many milestones and breakthroughs that have led to the technology we know today. Let's explore the evolution of AI and its journey from a theoretical idea to a practical tool integrated into everyday life.

1.2.1 The 1950s – AI's Early Foundations:
The idea of AI can be traced back to Alan Turing, a British mathematician who asked, "Can machines think?" In 1950, Turing introduced the Turing Test, a way to assess whether a machine could exhibit intelligent behaviour indistinguishable from that of a human.

The first significant step in AI research came in 1956 when computer scientist John McCarthy organised the Dartmouth Conference. This conference marked the official beginning of AI as a field of study, and it was here that the term "Artificial Intelligence" was coined.

1.2.2 The 1960s and 1970s – Early Developments:
During this period, researchers developed simple AI programs that could perform basic tasks, such as solving math problems or playing games. One well-known program from this era is ELIZA, which simulated conversations by mimicking a psychotherapist.

Despite these early successes, AI systems of this time were limited in their capabilities. Computers were not powerful enough to handle complex tasks, and AI researchers encountered many obstacles, leading to slower progress. This period of slowed AI development is sometimes called an "AI winter."

1.2.3 The 1980s – Rise of Expert Systems:
The 1980s saw a revival of interest in AI with the development of Expert Systems. These systems were designed to mimic the decision-making abilities of human experts in specific domains, such as medicine or engineering. Expert systems could diagnose diseases, offer legal advice, or troubleshoot mechanical issues by asking questions and comparing the answers to a Database of knowledge.

Although Expert Systems were helpful, they were limited to specific fields and couldn't adapt to new information or tasks outside their programming.

1.2.4 The 1990s – Machine Learning and Big Data:
AI research took a significant leap forward in the 1990s, thanks to the growth of the internet and the availability of vast amounts of Data, known as Big Data. Machine Learning (ML) algorithms became more effective because they could learn from this massive amount of Data.

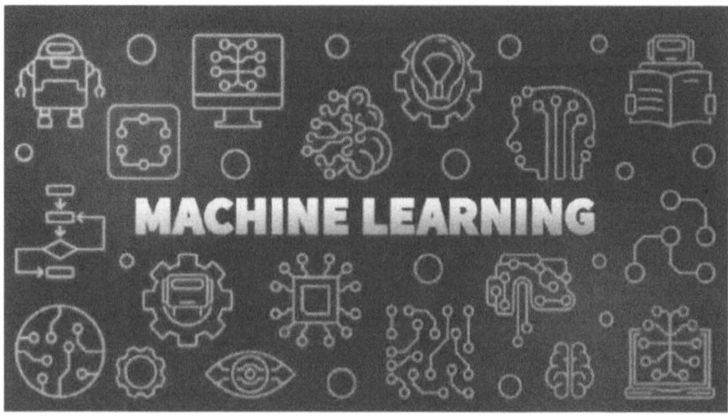

Search engines, like Google, began using Machine Learning to provide better search results by analysing user behaviour and preferences. Additionally, AI-powered recommendation systems, like those used by Amazon and Netflix, emerged during this period. These systems analyse user preferences and suggest products or movies based on past behaviour.

1.2.5 The 2000s and Beyond – Modern AI:

Today, AI has become more advanced and more integrated into our daily lives than ever before. Modern AI applications include virtual assistants, self-driving cars, and medical diagnostic tools. With the rise of Deep Learning—a more sophisticated form of Machine Learning—AI systems can now analyse large Datasets, recognize patterns, and make decisions with remarkable accuracy.

For example 2016, Google's AI system AlphaGo made headlines by defeating a world champion in the complex board game Go, demonstrating how far AI technology had come.
Artificial Intelligence (AI) has been a fascinating idea for many years. It started as a dream of making machines that could think like humans, and over time, it has grown into the unique technology we see today.

Key milestones in AI development:

Deep Blue (1997): IBM's Deep Blue became the first computer to defeat a world chess champion, Garry Kasparov, in a match. This event marked a significant milestone in AI, showcasing the potential of computers to perform tasks that require strategic thinking.

Watson (2011): IBM's Watson made headlines by winning the "Jeopardy!" quiz show against human champions. Watson's ability to understand Natural Language and Process vast amounts of information in real-time demonstrated the power of AI in processing and analysing Data.

AlphaGo (2016): Google DeepMind's AlphaGo defeated the world champion Go player, Lee Sedol, in a more complex game than chess. AlphaGo's success was due to its use of Deep Learning and Reinforcement Learning, highlighting AI's ability to learn and improve over time.

The future of AI: As AI continues to evolve, its future holds exciting possibilities, including the development of General AI and even Super AI, which could surpass Human Intelligence. Understanding the history of AI helps us appreciate how far we've come and what challenges and opportunities lie ahead.

1.3 Types of AI: Narrow, General, and Super AI

Based on its capabilities and potential, Artificial Intelligence can be classified into three main types: Narrow AI, General AI, and Super AI. Understanding these types helps clarify where current AI technology stands and what the future might hold.

1.3.1 Narrow AI (Weak AI):

Narrow AI refers to AI systems designed to perform specific tasks. These highly specialised systems cannot perform tasks outside of their programmed capabilities. Narrow AI is the most common form of AI we encounter daily.

Examples of Narrow AI:

Virtual assistants (e.g., Siri, Alexa): These AI systems can perform tasks like answering questions, setting reminders, and playing music, but they are limited to the specific functions they were programmed for.
Recommendation systems: AI-powered algorithms companies like Netflix, Amazon, and YouTube use to recommend content or products based on user behaviour and preferences.
Facial Recognition software: AI systems that recognise and authenticate individuals based on their facial features, commonly used in smartphones and security systems.

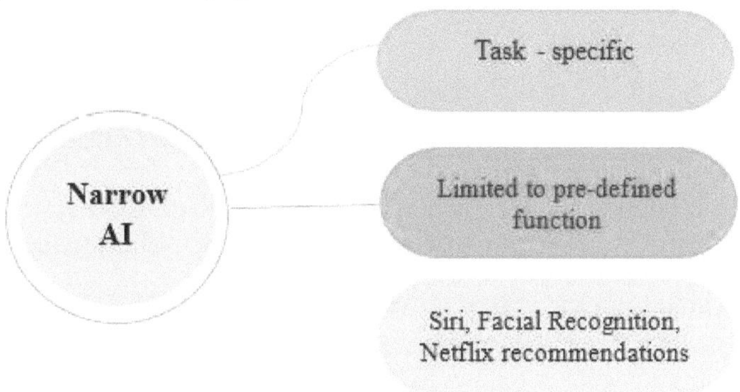

While Narrow AI is beneficial, it is restricted to performing only the tasks it was designed for and cannot adapt to new or unrelated tasks.

1.3.2 General AI (Strong AI):

General AI, also known as Strong AI, refers to machines that can perform any intellectual task that a human can do. Unlike Narrow AI, which is limited to specific domains, General AI can understand, learn, and apply knowledge across various fields.

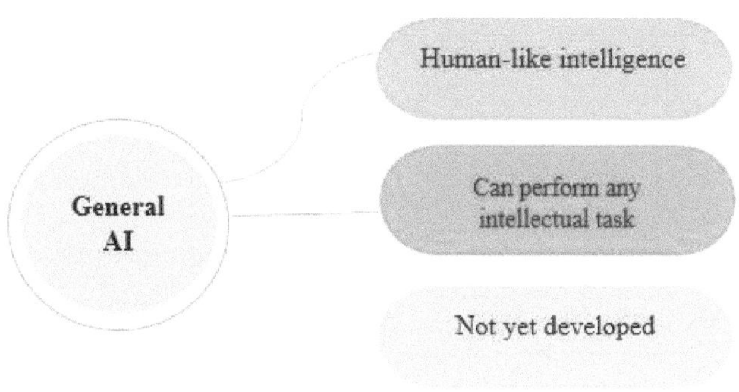

Characteristics of General AI:

General AI can solve complex problems and learn new tasks without explicit instructions or reprogramming.

It could apply its knowledge to various domains, such as Science, Art, and Engineering, in the same way humans can.
General AI is still a science fiction concept that does not currently exist. However, it remains a long-term goal for many AI researchers.

1.3.3 Super AI:

Super AI is a hypothetical form of AI that would surpass Human Intelligence in every aspect. While General AI could think like a human, Super AI would outperform humans in all intellectual tasks, including creativity, problem-solving, and decision-making.

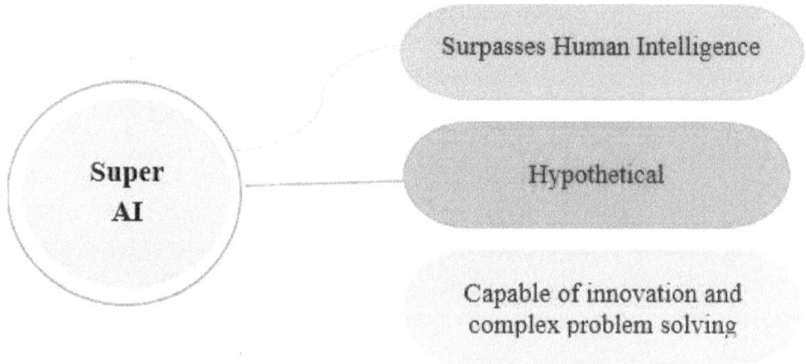

Potential capabilities of Super AI:

Super AI could solve complex global problems, such as climate change or disease eradication, faster and more efficiently than human scientists.
It could create new knowledge, make ground-breaking scientific discoveries, and innovate in ways humans cannot imagine.
Although Super AI is still theoretical, it raises important ethical questions. If AI systems become more intelligent than humans, how do we control them? What impact would this level of intelligence have on society?

1.4 Understanding Algorithms and Their Role in AI

An Algorithm is a fundamental concept in Computer Science and Artificial Intelligence. Simply put, an Algorithm is a set of instructions or steps a computer follows to complete a task. In AI, algorithms are the building blocks that allow machines to process information, learn from Data, and make decisions. These Algorithms make it possible for AI systems to perform tasks such as recognising speech, identifying images, and even playing games like chess or Go.

Let's explore algorithms, how they work in AI, and why they are essential for making AI systems effective.

1.4.1 What is an Algorithm?

An Algorithm is essentially a recipe for solving a problem. Just as a recipe for baking a cake involves steps (like mixing ingredients, baking in the oven, and decorating), an algorithm provides a step-by-step method for solving a problem or performing a task.

Algorithm

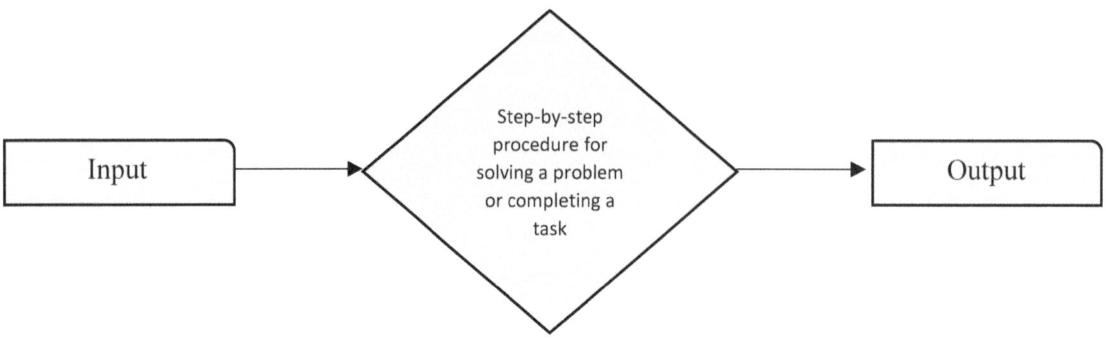

For example:

In mathematics, an algorithm might solve an equation by following specific rules.

An Algorithm could sort a list of numbers from smallest to most prominent in a computer program.

Algorithms are crucial in AI because they determine how a machine learns, makes predictions, and adapts to new situations.

1.4.2 The Role of Data in AI Algorithms

One of the primary functions of an AI Algorithm is to analyse Data. AI systems rely heavily on Data to make accurate predictions and decisions. This Data can come in the form of text, images, videos, or even sound. The Algorithm processes this Data and looks for patterns or trends that can help it understand and interpret the information.

For instance:

In Image Recognition, an AI system might be given thousands of labeled images of cats and dogs. The Algorithm analyses these images to determine the standard features of each category, such as the shape of the ears or the position of the eyes.

In a Language Processing task, the Algorithm could be trained on millions of text documents to understand how sentences are structured and what certain words mean in different contexts.

The more Data an AI system has, the better its Algorithm can learn, which leads to more accurate and reliable predictions.

1.4.3 How Algorithms learn: Training AI systems

One of the most critical roles of an AI Algorithm is to learn from Data. This process is known as Training. During the Training phase, the algorithm is exposed to a large Dataset and "learns" how to recognise patterns or solve problems based on the examples it has seen.

Here's how Training works:

Input Data: The AI system is given a large Dataset. In supervised learning (a common AI technique), this Data comes with labels. For example, a Dataset of images might be labeled with "cat" or "dog."

Algorithm Analysis: The Algorithm processes the Data and analyses the labeled examples. It looks for patterns, such as "cats usually have pointy ears" or "dogs typically have a certain fur texture."

Learning from Data: The algorithm then learns from these patterns. Over time, it becomes better at recognising cats and dogs, even when new images are shown that they have never seen before.

The more examples the Algorithm processes during training, the better it becomes at solving the task. This is the essence of Machine Learning, one of the most powerful applications of AI.

1.4.4 Types of AI Algorithms

Several Algorithms are used in AI, each suited to different kinds of tasks. Below are some of the most common types of AI algorithms:

Supervised Learning Algorithms: In Supervised Learning, the Algorithm is trained using labeled Data. The "supervision" comes from the system knowing the correct answer for each input during training.

Output

Labeled Data

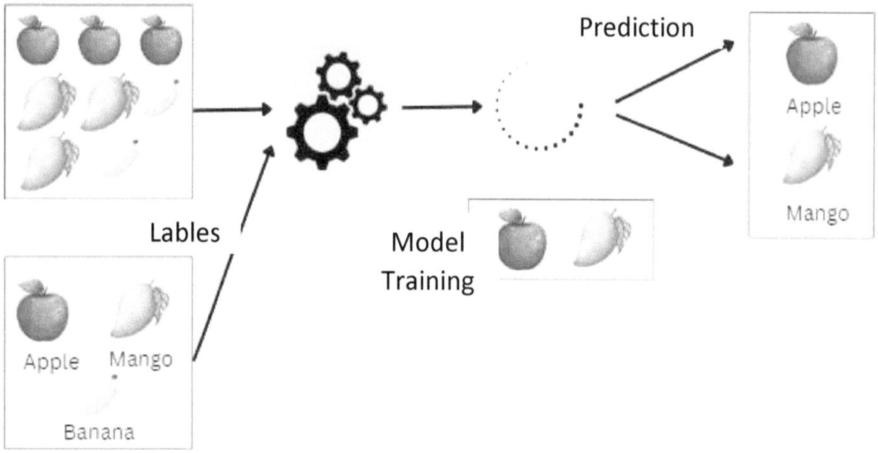

Example: An AI system that classifies images of animals might be trained using a Dataset where each image is labeled as "dog" or "cat." The Algorithm learns to associate certain features (like ear shape or fur pattern) with each label.

Use Case: Supervised learning is widely used in applications like image classification, voice recognition, and spam detection.

Unsupervised Learning Algorithms: The algorithm is not provided with labeled Data in unsupervised learning. Instead, patterns and relationships within the Data must be independently discovered.

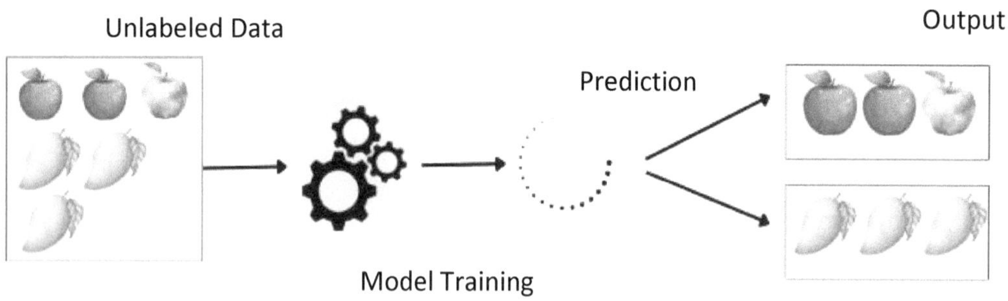

Example: A clustering algorithm might be used to group similar customers based on their purchasing behaviour, even though the Data does not have predefined labels.

Use Case: Unsupervised Learning is often used for tasks like Data Clustering, Anomaly Detection, and Recommendation Systems.

Reinforcement Learning Algorithms: In Reinforcement Learning, the Algorithm learns by interacting with its environment and receiving feedback in the form of rewards or penalties. This approach is often used when the AI needs to learn how to make a series of decisions to achieve a specific goal.

It's Banana

Wrong it's an Apple

Noted!

Reinforced Learning!

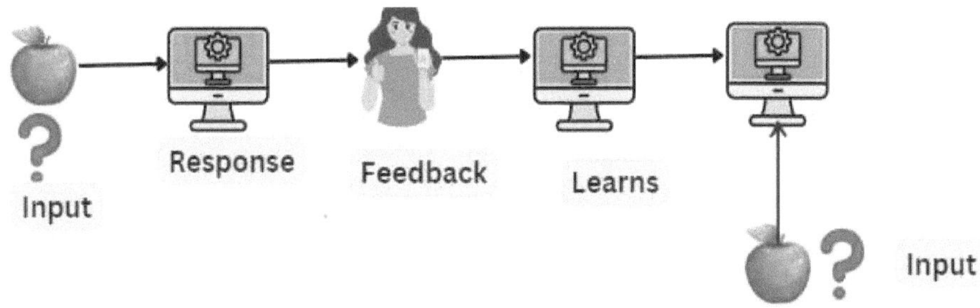

Example: In a video game, an AI Algorithm might learn to play by trial and error, receiving a reward for winning a game and a penalty for losing. Over time, the Algorithm adjusts its actions to maximise rewards.

Use Case: Reinforcement learning is used in robotics, gaming, and autonomous systems (like self-driving cars).

1.4.5 The Importance of Feedback in Algorithms

One key feature of AI Algorithms is their ability to improve over time through Feedback. Feedback is essential for AI systems because it allows the Algorithm to adjust its behaviour and become more accurate.

For instance, if an AI system classifies an image incorrectly (e.g., labelling a dog as a cat), it will receive feedback that tells it the prediction was wrong. This Feedback helps the Algorithm adjust its learning process so that it is less likely to make the same mistake in the future.

Feedback is essential in Reinforcement Learning. The AI learns by interacting with its environment and receiving rewards for successful actions or penalties for mistakes. Over time, the algorithm improves its decision-making ability by learning from its mistakes and maximising rewards.

1.4.6 Making Predictions and Decisions

Once an algorithm has been trained, it can start making predictions or decisions based on new, unseen Data. One of AI's most powerful aspects is the ability to generalise from past experiences and apply that knowledge to new situations.

For example:
A trained image recognition algorithm can accurately classify new images of cats and dogs, even if it has never seen those specific images before.

An AI system trained to detect spam emails can analyse new emails and decide whether they are spam based on patterns learned during training.
This process of making predictions from new Data is known as inference.

AI Algorithms and real-world applications
AI Algorithms are used in various real-world applications that make our lives easier and more efficient. Here are a few examples:

Healthcare: AI algorithms are used in medical imaging to help doctors identify diseases like cancer, etc. The Algorithm analyses images such as X-rays or MRIs, looking for patterns that indicate the presence of disease. AI is improving patient care and outcomes by assisting doctors in making quicker and more accurate diagnoses.

Transportation: Self-driving cars rely on AI Algorithms to navigate roads, avoid obstacles, and follow traffic rules. These algorithms process Data from sensors, cameras, and GPS systems to make real-time steering, braking, and accelerating decisions.

Entertainment: Streaming platforms like Netflix and YouTube use AI Algorithms to recommend movies, TV shows, and videos. These algorithms analyse user behaviour (viewing history and preferences) to suggest content users will likely enjoy.

Finance: AI algorithms are used for fraud detection in the financial industry. These algorithms can analyse transaction Data to detect unusual patterns indicating fraudulent activity, helping financial institutions protect their customers.

1.4.7 The Future of AI Algorithms

As AI continues to evolve, so do the Algorithms that power it. Researchers are constantly improving AI Algorithms to make them faster, more accurate, and more adaptable. Future AI Algorithms may be able to handle even more complex tasks, such as solving global challenges like climate change or creating new scientific breakthroughs.

One area of ongoing research is explainable AI (XAI), which focuses on creating AI systems that can explain their decisions in a way that humans can understand. This is important for building trust in AI systems, especially in fields like healthcare or law, where the consequences of AI decisions can be significant.

1.5 Summary

AI mimics Human Intelligence in performing tasks, learning, and making decisions.
Narrow AI specialises in specific tasks; General AI aims for human-like intelligence; Super AI is a theoretical concept surpassing Human Intelligence.
Algorithms enable AI to process Data, recognise patterns, and make decisions.
AI systems learn from large Datasets and improve over time through feedback.
Types of AI algorithms include Supervised, Unsupervised, and Reinforcement Learning.
Real-world AI applications include healthcare diagnosis, self-driving cars, and content recommendations.
The future of AI focuses on improving accuracy and developing explainable AI systems for better trust and transparency.

1.6 Glossary

Artificial Intelligence (AI): The simulation of Human Intelligence by machines.
Narrow AI: AI that performs specific tasks.
General AI: A Theoretical AI that would have human-like reasoning abilities.
Super AI: A Hypothetical AI that would surpass Human Intelligence.
Algorithm: A set of instructions for solving a problem or completing a task.

Machine Learning (ML): AI that learns from Data without being explicitly programmed.
Supervised Learning: A type of learning where the algorithm is trained with Labeled Data.
Unsupervised Learning: A type of learning where the algorithm finds patterns in Unlabeled Data.
Reinforcement Learning: A learning method where AI improves by receiving rewards or penalties for actions.
Big Data: Large volumes of Data are used to train AI systems.
Deep Learning: An advanced form of Machine Learning that uses Neural Networks to process large Datasets.

1.7 Exercise

Exercise 1 – Choose the correct answer from the given options.

1. What does AI stand for?
a) Artificial Intelligence
b) Automated Intelligence
c) Advanced Intelligence
d) Active Intelligence

2. Which of the following is an example of Narrow AI?
a) A system that plays chess
b) A system that can perform any human task
c) A self-driving car
d) Both a and c

3. What does an Algorithm do in AI?
a) It improves Human Intelligence
b) It provides instructions for solving tasks
c) It stores Data
d) It makes computers faster

4. When did AI research officially begin?
a) 1956
b) 1960
c) 1990
d) 2005

5. What does Reinforcement Learning involve?
a) Labeled Data
b) Unlabeled Data
c) Rewards and Penalties
d) None of the above

Exercise 2 – Check if the sentence is true or false.

1. AI can mimic human behaviour. ....
2. General AI currently exists and is widely used. ....
3. Algorithms in AI can learn from Data and improve over time. ....
4. Narrow AI can perform tasks beyond its programming. ....
5. Machine Learning algorithms rely on large amounts of Data to function. ....

Exercise 3 – Fill the blank space with the correct word.

1. AI systems learn by being trained on large ....
2. .... AI refers to machines that can perform specific tasks only.
3. Super AI is a .... form of AI that surpasses Human Intelligence.
4. .... learning uses rewards and penalties to teach AI.
5. The .... Conference marked the beginning of AI as a formal field.

Exercise 4 – Match word or phrase in Column A with Column B.

Column A	Column B
1. Narrow AI	a. Mimics specific human tasks
2. Supervised Learning	b. Uses Labeled Data
3. Reinforcement Learning	c. Learns through rewards and penalties

4. Dartmouth Conference	d. Official start of the AI field
5. Facial Recognition	e. An example of Narrow AI

Exercise 5 – Answer the following questions in your own words (3-4 lines).

1. What is the difference between Narrow AI and General AI?
2. Describe the concept of Machine Learning in AI.
3. Explain the importance of Feedback in AI Algorithms.
4. What is Supervised Learning?
5. What is the significance of computing power in AI?

Exercise 6 – Use the given clues below and complete the crossword.

Across:

2. AI that surpasses Human Intelligence.
3. AI that can perform specific tasks.
5. A set of instructions for solving a problem in AI.
6. A branch of AI that allows machines to interpret images.
8. A subset of AI that learns from Data.

Down:

1. AI learning through Labeled Data.
4. The official start of AI research in 1956.
7. AI system that recognises faces.

1.8 Project Work

Link: https://www.youtube.com/playlist?list=PLzlh_31VWEFrfKeEkUgyw7JAEHJ1tQlvx

QR Code:

Creating a simple chatbot using Scratch

To build a simple chatbot using Scratch, a block-based visual programming language, and learn how to make the chatbot interact with users by responding to inputs.

1.9 Group Discussion

Link: https://www.youtube.com/playlist?list=PLzlh_31VWEFoIf-R5jloFNPxidWkPN4cf

QR Code:

The future of AI: Opportunities and Challenges

Scenario: A teacher moderates a Group Discussion among students on the future of Artificial Intelligence. The focus is on how AI could impact various fields, such as education, healthcare, and entertainment, along with potential Ethical Challenges and job losses due to automation.

Guiding questions for the above group discussion:

1. What opportunities does AI present for future generations?
2. How can AI improve industries like healthcare and education?
3. What risks and challenges are associated with AI, such as privacy concerns or job displacement?
4. How can humans ensure that AI is developed ethically and safely?

1.10 Case Study

Link:https://www.youtube.com/playlist?list=PLzlh_31VWEFoSpfUhWA6BpZTwy4nBgvNm

QR Code:

AI in smart cities: Improving urban living

Analyse how AI is being used to improve the efficiency of services and the quality of life in smart cities.

Scenario: A major city has started implementing AI-powered systems to manage traffic, reduce energy consumption, and enhance public safety. The AI systems analyse Data from sensors placed across the city to make real-time decisions, such as optimising traffic lights to reduce congestion or monitoring energy usage to avoid waste.

Exploring AI: A Fun Chat Between Friends in the Park

Exactly! My phone's face recognition is all thanks to those algorithms getting smarter with more data.
Yeah, and algorithms are what make AI work. They help it learn by following data, like solving puzzles really fast.

Maybe clean my room! Now that's the kind of AI I want.
AI is everywhere now. Imagine what it'll do in the future.

Same here! Let's see if AI helps us ace the test.
Haha, me too! I'm excited for the next AI class!

1.11 Fun Activity

CODING GAME

BLOCK CODING

Name: ....

- Guide the rabbit to the carrot using block codes.

CODING AREA

Start

Stop

CODE BLOCKS

Turn LEFT ←

Turn UP ↑

Turn RIGHT →

Turn DOWN ↓

Repeat

Move Steps

1 2

3 4

5 6

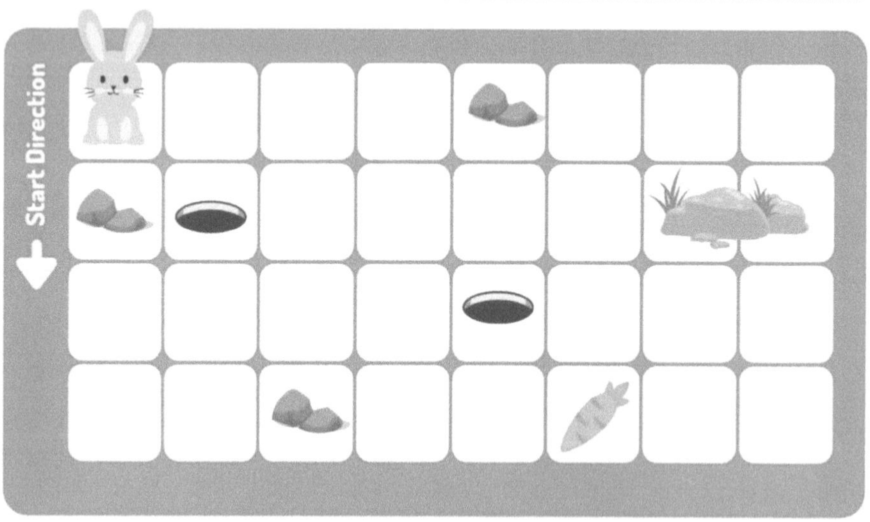

CODING GAME

BLOCK CODING

INSTRUCTIONS

- Guide the rabbit to the carrot using block codes.

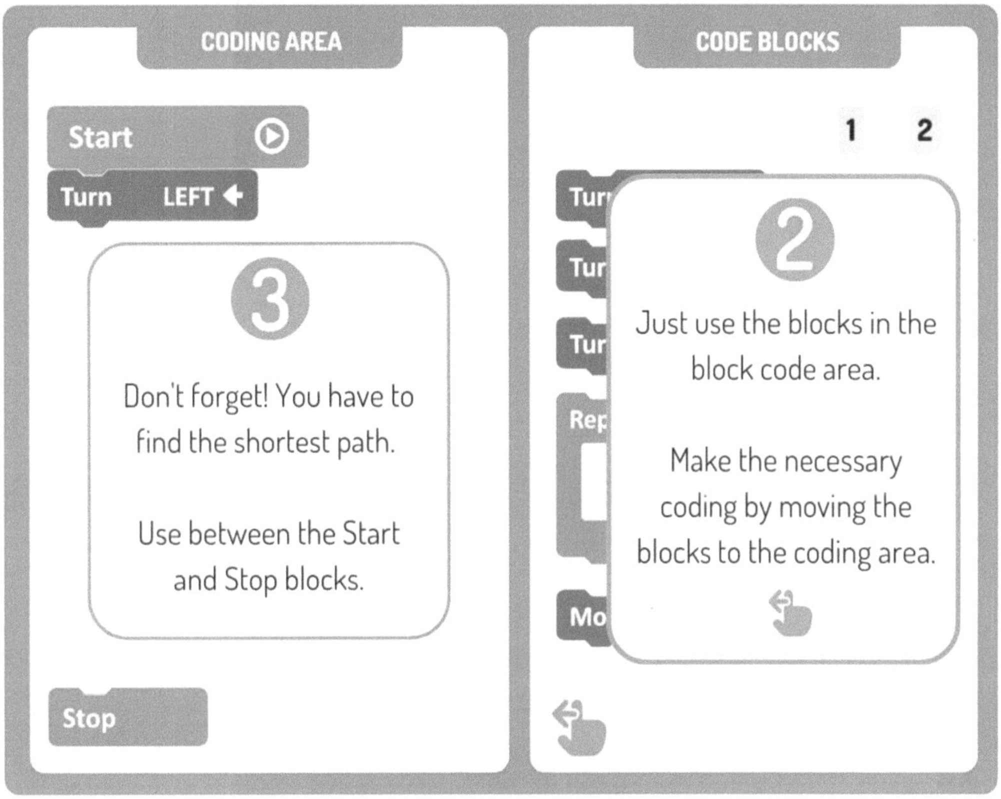

Chapter-1
Test Paper
Advanced Concepts in Artificial Intelligence

Time Duration: 40 Minutes **Maximum Marks: 30**

General Instructions:

1. This paper consists of twelve questions and is divided into two sections: A and B.
2. All questions are compulsory.
3. Section A comprises MCQs, Fill in the blanks, True or False, and One word of one mark each.
4. Section B comprises answering the following questions with three marks each.

SECTION-A

I - Choose the correct answer from the given options. **(1 X 2 = 2 marks)**

1. Which of the following is an example of AI?
   a) Algorithm
   b) Voice assistants
   c) Database
   d) Computer Network

2. What kind of Data does supervised learning use?
   a) Unlabeled Data
   b) Incorrect Data
   c) Labeled Data
   d) Random Data

II - Fill in the blank space with the correct word. **(1 X 2 = 2 marks)**

1. .... uses Labeled Data for Training AI models.
2. AI is powered by .... and algorithms to function effectively.

III - Check if the sentence is true or false. **(1 X 2 = 2 marks)**

1. AI can recognise objects in images. ....
2. Super AI is widely used today. ....

IV - Write the answer in one word. **(1 X 2 = 2 marks)**

1. What does AI stand for?
2. What kind of learning uses Labeled Data?

SECTION-B

V - Answer the following questions in your own words. **(3 X 4 = 12 marks)**

1. Explain the difference between Supervised and Unsupervised Learning.
2. What is the importance of feedback in AI?
3. How does AI benefit the healthcare industry?
4. What is Reinforcement Learning in AI?

Answer

Exercise 1- 1. a) 2. d) 3. b) 4. a) 5. c)
Exercise 2- 1. True 2. False 3. True 4. False 5. True
Exercise 3- 1. Datasets 2. Narrow 3. Hypothetical 4. Reinforcement 5. Dartmouth
Exercise 4 - 1. a 2. b 3. c 4. d 5. e
Exercise 5 - 1. Supervised 2. Super 3. Narrow 4. Dartmouth 5. Algorithm 6. Computer 7. Facial 8. Machine

Online Resources

Online Exam Paper Link:
Link: https://forms.gle/QH1DaboxWEU9AVECA
QR Code:

Chapter 1 Videos Link:
Link: https://www.youtube.com/playlist?list=PLzlh_31VWEFr-G3lJ7CBwGNDP4vmVyUlY
QR Code:

More Sample Test Paper

Chapter 1 Test Paper – 1 Link:
Link: https://forms.gle/NHeHL2WSWzFtPbgo6
QR Code:

Chapter 1 Test Paper – 2 Link:
Link: https://forms.gle/5pwPjwTBiF8XvarB9
QR Code:

Chapter 1 Test Paper – 3 Link:
Link: https://forms.gle/49Gaa6zqgPzQzwEg6
QR Code:

Chapter 1 Test Paper – 4 Link:
Link: https://forms.gle/4rroywicbxt4HueZ9
QR Code:

Exam Tips

Read the questions carefully before answering to avoid mistakes.

Chapter 2: Human-Machine Interaction

Learning Objectives

Understand HMI and its significance.
Describe HMI's evolution from CLI to BCI.
Identify types of HMI: GUI, Touch, Voice, Gesture, AR/VR.
Recognize key components: Input/Output Devices, Software, Algorithms.
Explore future HMI trends: Natural Interaction, Emotional Intelligence, Holographic Interfaces.
Understand Human-Centered Design (HCD) for user-friendly tech.
Discuss ethical concerns: Privacy, Security, Fairness.

Human-Machine Interaction (HMI) refers to the interaction between humans and machines, where machines can be anything from computers and robots to mobile devices and intelligent appliances. As technology has evolved, how we communicate and interact with these machines has become more advanced. This interaction is critical because it determines how easily and effectively we use technology daily.

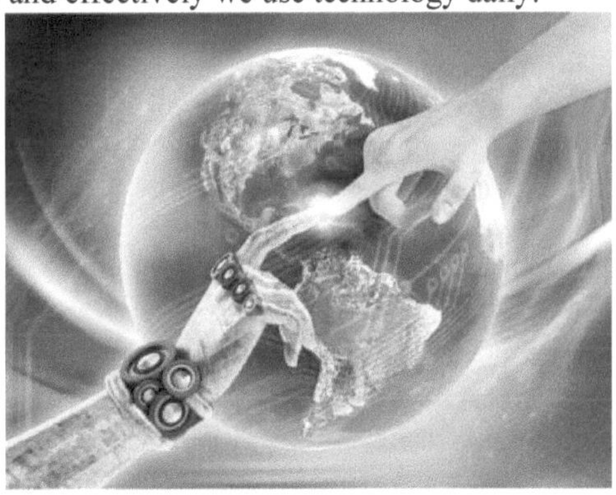

HMI has significant implications in almost every industry, from healthcare and education to entertainment and manufacturing. The goal of HMI is not just to make machines functional but to make them easy and intuitive to use. The better the interaction between humans and machines, the more efficiently we can perform tasks, solve problems, and enhance our daily lives.

2.1 History and Evolution of Human-Machine Interaction

The development of Human-Machine Interaction is a fascinating journey that began with the earliest computers and continues to evolve today. Let's explore the key milestones in the evolution of HMI and how it has shaped modern technology.

2.1.1 The Early Beginnings – Command Line Interfaces (1950s–1970s):

The first interactions between humans and computers were through Command-Line Interfaces (CLI). This was a primary method where users would type commands into a terminal, and the computer would respond with text-based output. The famous ENIAC computer, one of the first general-purpose computers, required users to physically switch wires and input commands manually.

Command-line interfaces require users to have specialised knowledge of programming and specific commands. For instance, the user had to type a particular command and know the correct syntax to perform a simple task like copying a file. As a result, these early systems were not accessible to the general public and were mainly used by scientists, engineers, and computer specialists.

Example:
Early UNIX operating systems allowed users to manipulate files by entering commands like cp (copy) or rm (remove). While powerful, these commands required memorisation and technical expertise.

2.1.2 Graphical User Interfaces (1980s–1990s):
In the 1980s, a significant breakthrough in HMI came with the development of Graphical User Interfaces (GUI). Instead of typing commands, users could interact with computers using graphical elements like icons, buttons, and menus. This made computers much easier to use and opened the door for personal computing.

Apple Macintosh (introduced in 1984) and Microsoft Windows (released in 1985) were pioneers in developing GUI systems. These operating systems allowed users to point and click with a mouse, making computers more accessible to everyday people. GUIs are still the dominant form of interaction on desktop computers and laptops today.

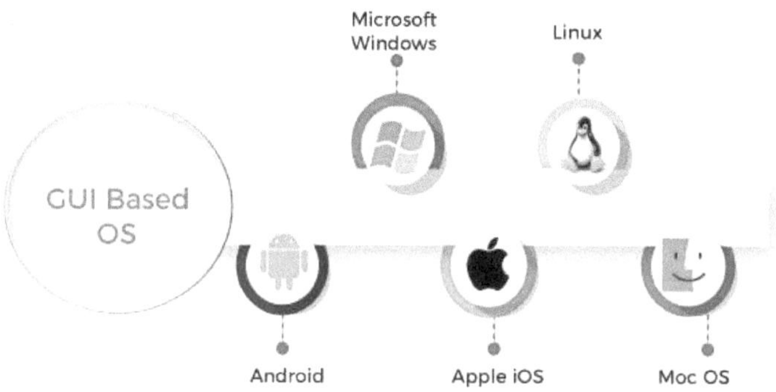

Example:
The Macintosh GUI popularised using a mouse to click on icons, drag files, and open folders, transforming computing into a visual, user-friendly experience.

2.1.3 Touch Interfaces and Mobile Devices (2000s):
The 2000s witnessed a revolution in Human-Machine Interaction with the introduction of touch interfaces. Touchscreens allow users to interact with devices directly by touching the display. Apple's launch of the iPhone in 2007 transformed the mobile industry by introducing a fully touch-based interface that removed the need for physical buttons.

Touch-based interaction became intuitive, allowing users to tap, swipe, and pinch to navigate apps and webpages. Tablets, smartphones, and even some laptops now use touchscreens, making interaction more seamless and user-friendly. It became so popular that even ATMs and self-service kiosks adopted touch interfaces for user input.

Example:
Microsoft's Kinect used depth-sensing cameras to track body movements, allowing players to control games through gestures without needing a controller.

2.1.4 Voice and Gesture Interfaces (2010s–Present):

Voice-based interaction has emerged as one of the most significant advancements in HMI. With the advent of Natural Language Processing (NLP), devices like Amazon Alexa, Google Assistant, and Apple Siri became household names. Voice assistants allow users to give voice commands to devices, which can perform tasks such as answering questions, setting reminders, or controlling smart home devices.

At the same time, gesture-based interaction became popular in gaming consoles, such as Microsoft Kinect and Nintendo Wii, where users could control the system using body movements. Gesture recognition enables users to control devices without physically touching them, adding another interaction layer.

2.1.5 The Future – Brain-Computer Interfaces:

Brain-Computer Interfaces (BCI) represent the next frontier in Human-Machine Interaction. BCI systems enable direct communication between the brain and a machine, allowing users to control devices using brain signals. Companies like Neuralink are actively researching BCIs, which have the potential to revolutionise fields like medicine, allowing people with disabilities to control devices or communicate more easily. BCIs may also extend into everyday use, making interaction faster and more intuitive than ever before.

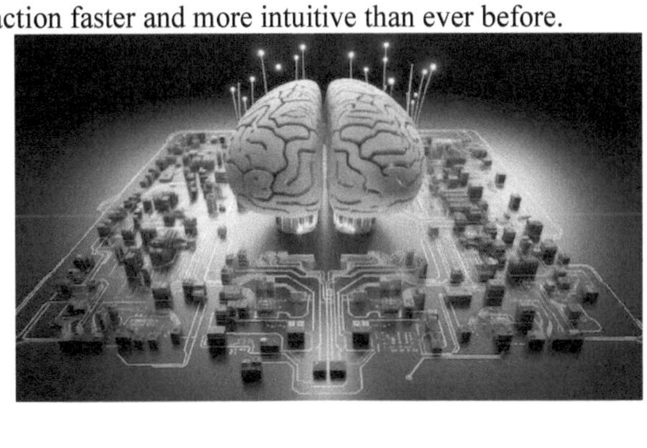

2.2 Components and Stages of Human-Machine Interaction

Human-Machine Interaction is a complex process that involves multiple components working together to enable seamless communication between humans and machines. Each stage of this interaction is essential to ensuring that users can efficiently perform tasks on the device.

2.2.1 Input Devices: Input devices are the starting point of Human-Machine Interaction. They allow users to provide Data or Commands to the machine. Standard input devices include:
Keyboards and Mouse: These are used for typing and pointing in traditional desktop setups.
Touchscreens: These are used in smartphones, tablets, and modern laptops to interact directly with the display.
Voice Recognition Systems: These are used in voice assistants like Siri and Alexa to interpret spoken commands.
Gesture Sensors: Devices like Microsoft Kinect use sensors to track body movements, translating them into commands for games or applications.
Input devices serve as humans' primary means of sending instructions to machines.

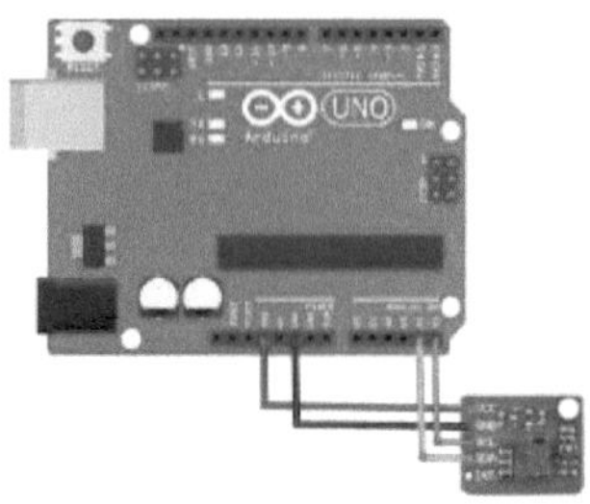

2.2.2 Output Devices: Output devices are responsible for delivering feedback from the machine to the user. These include:
Monitors and Screens: Display visual content such as text, images, and videos.
Speakers and Headphones: Provide audio feedback such as music, voice, or system notifications.
Haptic Feedback Devices: Found in smartphones and gaming controllers, haptics provide physical sensations like vibration to inform the user about system events.

Output devices close the communication loop by allowing the user to receive responses from the machine.

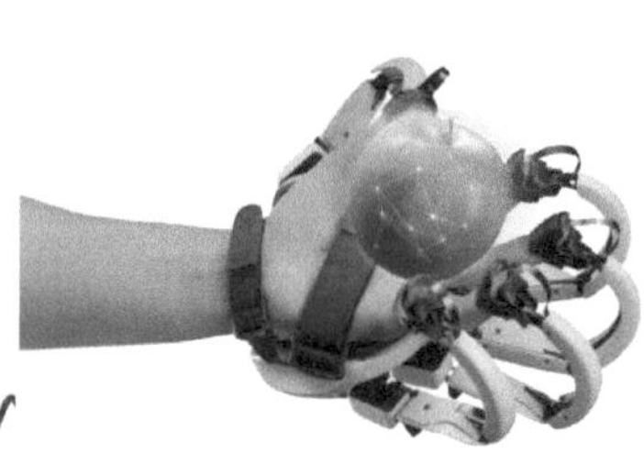

2.2.3 Software and Algorithms: Software is the bridge that connects user input with machine output. When a user interacts with a device, the software processes that input using algorithms, determining how the machine responds. For example:
The algorithm analyses the user's query in a search engine and provides relevant search results.
In a voice assistant, the algorithm processes the spoken command and executes the task (e.g., playing music or setting an alarm).

2.2.4 tages of Interaction: The interaction between humans and machines can be broken down into stages:
Input stage: The user provides input via an input device, such as typing on a keyboard or speaking to a virtual assistant.
Processing stage: The machine processes the input using software and algorithms, analysing the information to determine the appropriate action.
Output stage: The machine delivers feedback or acts, such as displaying search results or answering a question.
Feedback stage: The user receives the output and may provide additional input, leading to a continuous interaction loop.
These stages are the foundation of any Human-Machine Interaction and ensure the system functions smoothly.

2.3 Different types of Human-Machine Interaction

As technology has progressed, different types of human-machine interaction have emerged. Each type is suited to different devices and user needs. Here are some of the most common forms of HMI:

2.3.1 Command-Line Interaction:

In the earliest computers, users interacted with machines through text-based Command-Line Interfaces (CLI). This method involved typing specific commands to perform tasks. CLIs require technical knowledge, as users need to understand syntax and language to operate the system.

Example: Early programming languages like BASIC and UNIX required users to type commands to perform basic operations like copying files or running programs.

2.3.2 Graphical User Interfaces (GUI):

Graphical User Interfaces (GUIs) represent a significant leap in HMI. GUIs use icons, windows, and menus that users can interact with using a mouse or touchpad. This visual approach is much more intuitive and user-friendly than Command-Line Interaction.

Example: The desktop environment in operating systems like Windows or macOS, where users can click icons and drag files.

2.3.3 Touch-Based Interaction:

Touchscreens introduced a more direct and intuitive way to interact with machines. Instead of relying on physical buttons or a mouse, users can touch, swipe, and pinch the screen to perform tasks. Touch interaction is widely used in smartphones, tablets, and public kiosks.

Example: Smartphones and tablets like the iPhone and iPad allow users to control apps and navigate using touch gestures.

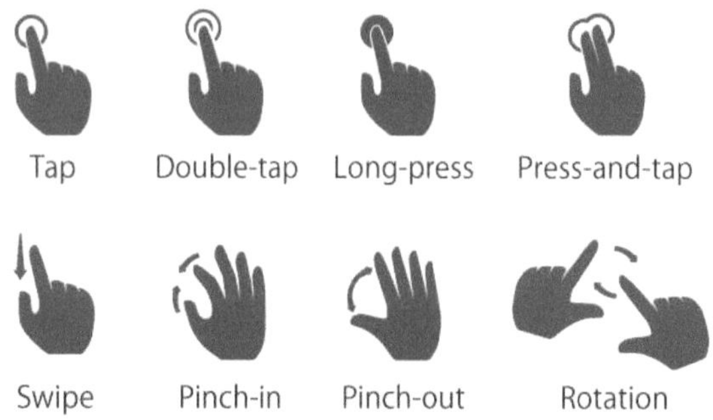

2.3.4 Voice-Based Interaction:

Voice-based interaction allows users to control devices using natural language. Virtual assistants like Siri, Alexa, and Google Assistant have become increasingly popular because they can perform tasks using voice commands. This form of interaction is proper for hands-free operation and enhances accessibility.

Example: Users can ask a voice assistant to play music, set alarms, or provide weather updates simply by speaking.

2.3.5 Gesture-Based Interaction:

Gesture-Based systems allow users to interact with devices by moving their hands or body. Devices like Microsoft Kinect use sensors to detect body movements, enabling users to control systems through gestures. Gesture recognition is also used in smart TVs, gaming systems, and AR/VR applications.

Example: The Nintendo Wii allows users to control games using physical gestures, such as swinging a tennis racket or bowling.

2.3.6 Augmented Reality (AR) and Virtual Reality (VR) Interaction:
Augmented Reality and Virtual Reality provide more immersive types of interaction. In AR, users interact with digital elements that are overlaid into the real world. In VR, users are placed in a completely virtual environment to interact with virtual objects and spaces.

Example: Pokémon GO is an AR game where digital Pokémon appear in the real world through the user's phone camera. In VR, users can explore virtual worlds using headsets like the Oculus Rift.

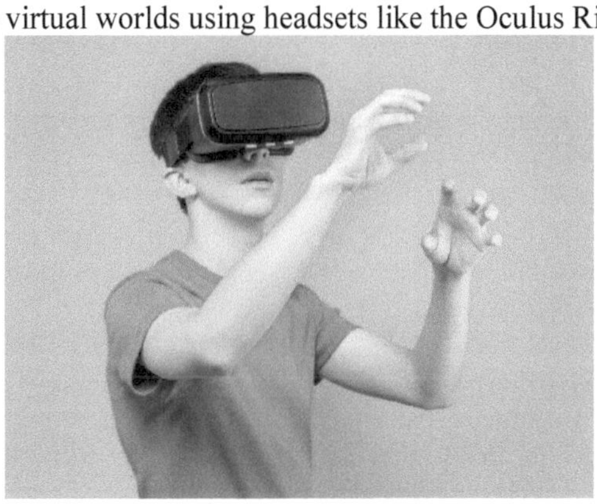

2.3.7 Brain-Computer Interfaces (BCI):
BCIs represent a futuristic interaction in which users control devices directly through brain signals. Although still in the experimental phase, BCIs hold great potential, especially for people with disabilities who may not be able to use traditional input methods. BCI technology could one day allow users to interact with machines purely by thinking about what they want to do.

Example: Early prototypes of BCIs have allowed users to control robotic limbs or computer cursors using brain activity.

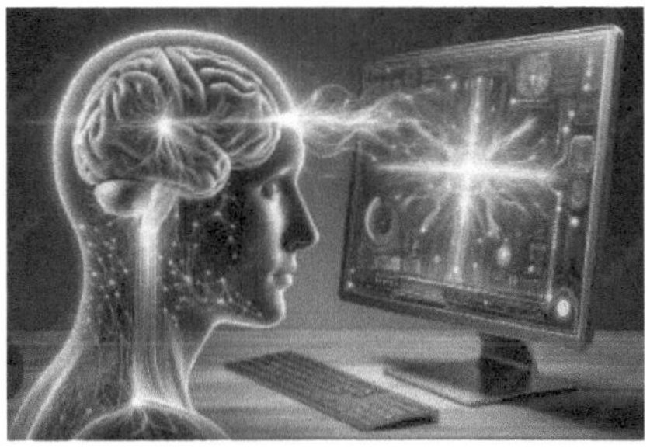

2.4 The Future of Human-Machine Interaction
As technology advances, the future of Human-Machine Interaction is becoming more exciting and promising. Several trends and innovations are shaping the next generation of HMI systems:

2.4.1 Natural Interaction:

Future HMI aims to make interaction as natural and intuitive as possible. This includes improving voice and gesture recognition and creating interfaces that adapt to human behaviour. Devices may become more responsive to subtle cues, such as tone of voice or facial expressions, making interactions smoother and more human-like.

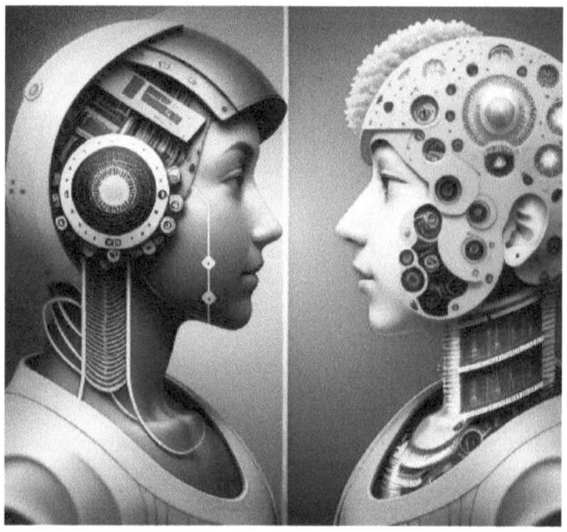

2.4.2 Immersive Experiences with AR/VR:

Augmented Reality and Virtual Reality are expected to become more advanced, allowing users to experience digital environments that feel real. These technologies will be used in education, gaming, medicine, and architecture, where users can visualise and interact with virtual spaces before they are built.

2.4.3 Brain-Computer Interfaces (BCI):

Brain-Computer Interfaces (BCIs) will continue to develop, allowing humans to control devices with their thoughts. BCIs could improve accessibility for people with disabilities, and in the future, they might be used for everyday tasks, making technology even more seamless.

2.4.4 Emotional Intelligence in Machines:

The future may also see the rise of machines capable of detecting and responding to human emotions. AI systems could analyse facial expressions, voice tone, or body language to determine how users feel and adjust their responses accordingly. This could make Human-Machine Interaction more empathetic and responsive to users' emotional states.

2.4.5 Ethical Considerations and Privacy:

As machines become more integrated into our lives, ethical concerns will become more prominent. Issues such as Data Privacy, Security, and the potential misuse of AI technologies must be addressed. Developers must ensure that future HMI systems prioritise user safety and fairness, while governments may need to establish regulations to protect users from harm.

2.4.6 Holographic and 3D Interfaces:

In the future, we may see more Holographic Interfaces where users interact with 3D projections of digital content. These systems could replace traditional screens, allowing users to engage with floating images and objects in real time. This could revolutionise the way we interact with digital information, making it feel more tangible and immersive.

2.5 Importance of Human-Centered Design in HMI

A crucial aspect of modern Human-Machine Interaction is the concept of Human-Centered Design (HCD). This approach focuses on designing technology that meets users' needs, capabilities, and limitations rather than forcing users to adapt. HCD ensures that machines are user-friendly, accessible, and efficient, improving the overall experience.

Principles of Human-Centered Design:

User needs first: The design process begins by understanding users' needs. Designers research what users expect from a machine or system and how they interact with it.

Feedback and Iteration: Prototypes are tested with users, and their feedback is used to refine the design. This ensures that the final product is intuitive and efficient.

Ease of use: A machine should be easy to learn and use, even for people who are not technically skilled. The goal is to reduce frustration and make the technology accessible to many users.

Flexibility: Machines should be designed to accommodate different user preferences and environments. For example, a system that works well in an office setting should also be adaptable to use at home or in public spaces.

Example of Human-Centered Design in HMI:

Smartphones: Modern smartphones are designed to be accessible to users of all ages and skill levels. Features like voice recognition, gesture control, and customisable interfaces ensure that smartphones meet the diverse needs of their users.

2.6 Summary

Human-Machine Interaction (HMI) refers to how humans interact with machines, including computers, robots, and smart devices.

HMI has evolved significantly, from Command-Line Interfaces (CLI) in the 1950s to Graphical User Interfaces (GUI), touchscreens, voice assistants, and gesture-based systems.

The components of HMI include input devices (keyboard, mouse, touchscreen, etc.), output devices (monitors, speakers, etc.), and software that processes user commands.

There are several types of HMI, including touch-based, voice-based, gesture-based, AR/VR, and Brain-Computer Interfaces (BCI).

The future of HMI will focus on natural interaction, immersive AR/VR experiences, BCIs, and machines that can detect and respond to human emotions.

Human-Centered Design (HCD) ensures that technology is created to meet users' needs, making machines easy to use and adaptable.

Ethical concerns such as Data Privacy, Security, and AI's impact on society must be considered in the development of future HMI systems.

2.7 Glossary

Human-Machine Interaction (HMI): The communication & interaction between humans & machines.
Command-Line Interface (CLI): A text-based interface where users type commands to interact with a computer.
Graphical User Interface (GUI): An interface that uses graphical elements like icons and windows to facilitate interaction.
Touchscreen: A display that allows users to interact by touching the screen.
Voice Assistant: A software that uses voice recognition to perform tasks based on spoken commands (e.g., Siri, Alexa).
Gesture-Based Interaction: A form of interaction where users control machines using body movements.
Augmented Reality (AR): Technology that overlays digital elements in the real world.
Virtual Reality (VR): A fully immersive digital environment that users can interact with.
Brain-Computer Interface (BCI): A system that enables direct communication between the brain and a machine.
Human-Centered Design (HCD): A design philosophy that focuses on creating technology that meets user needs and is easy to use.

2.8 Exercise

Exercise 1 – Choose the correct answer from the given options.

1. What does HMI stand for?
a) Human-Machine Interface
b) Human-Machine Interaction
c) Human Media Interaction
d) Hybrid Machine Intelligence

2. Which interface uses graphical elements like icons and menus?
a) CLI
b) BCI
c) GUI
d) AR

3. Which device interprets spoken commands in HMI?
a) Keyboard
b) Voice Assistant
c) Monitor
d) Mouse

4. What does BCI enable?
a) Communication through typing
b) Control via brain signals
c) Gesture-based control
d) Virtual environments

5. Which technology overlays digital elements in the real world?
a) VR

b) CLI
c) AR
d) GUI

Exercise 2 –Fill the blank space with the correct word.

1. The full form of HMI is ....
2. A .... allows users to control devices using brain signals.
3. Voice assistants like Alexa use .... recognition for commands.
4. .... interfaces are widely used in smartphones and tablets.
5. In the future, machines may have .... intelligence to detect emotions.

Exercise 3 – Check if the sentence is true or false.

1. AR stands for Augmented Reality. ....
2. Command-Line Interface (CLI) is an advanced, user-friendly interface. ....
3. BCI allows communication between the brain and devices. ....
4. GUI uses text-based commands to operate devices. ....
5. Ethical concerns like Data Privacy are important in HMI. ....

Exercise 4 – Match each word or phrase in Column A with Column B.

Column A	Column B
1. GUI	a. Brain signals
2. BCI	b. Voice commands
3. Voice Assistant	c. Clickable icons and menus
4. Augmented Reality (AR)	d. Digital elements overlaid
5. Haptic Feedback	e. Physical vibrations

Exercise 5 – Answer the following questions in your own words (3-4 lines).

1. What is Human-Machine Interaction (HMI)?
2. What is the difference between GUI and CLI?
3. How does a Brain-Computer Interface (BCI) work?
4. What is the role of voice assistants in HMI?
5. What are the ethical concerns related to HMI?

Exercise 6 – Choose the word that best describes the picture and write the word in the blank.

Monitor Printer Video Webcam Mouse Speakers
Router Keyboard CPU USB

Exercise 7 - Create a flowchart showing the stages of Human-Machine Interaction (HMI). Your flowchart should include the following stages.

Input Stage: How does the user give a command or input to the machine? (e.g., typing, speaking, touching)
Processing Stage: How does the machine process this input? (e.g., using algorithms, speech recognition, or data processing)
Output Stage: How does the machine provide feedback or perform an action? (e.g., displaying information, playing sound, performing a task)
Feedback Stage: How does the user respond to the machine's output, if necessary? (e.g., providing more input, reacting to the feedback)

Example: If you are using a voice assistant, the flowchart might look like this:
Input: The user gives a voice command.
Processing: The machine processes the voice command using speech recognition.
Output: The machine responds with a voice or performs an action.
Feedback: The user provides additional input if needed.

Link:https://www.youtube.com/playlist?list=PLzlh_31VWEFo8p5x9wBy09NZP2imm36Q2

QR Code:

2.9 Project Work

Building a Human-Machine Interaction System

This project will design and build a Human-Machine Interaction (HMI) System using Scratch. It will allow students to explore the different components, stages, types, and future possibilities of HMI and simulate real-world applications using block-based programming.

2.10 Group Discussion

Link: https://www.youtube.com/playlist?list=PLzlh_31VWEFp8cvy5vsOOlfEikO_UPCKO

QR Code:

The Future of Human-Machine Interaction:

The group discussion is designed to engage students in a thoughtful conversation about the future of HMI. The primary objective is to explore opportunities and challenges presented by emerging technologies such as Brain-Computer Interfaces (BCI) and emotionally intelligent machines. The discussion also aims to highlight ethical concerns, including Data Privacy and the role of machines in daily life. Students will develop critical thinking skills by debating the pros and cons of these advancements.

2.11 Case Study

Link: https://www.youtube.com/playlist?list=PLzlh_31VWEFr3raxRjWZbcZfqDXThQE5f

QR Code:

Improving HMI for Accessibility

Scenario: A company is developing a new tablet designed for people with disabilities. The goal is to make the tablet as accessible as possible, ensuring that people with visual, hearing, and physical disabilities can use it without difficulty.

Tasks:

- Identify the challenges that people with disabilities might face when using standard touch-based interfaces.
- Suggest solutions using different types of HMI (e.g., voice-based, gesture-based, or haptic feedback) to improve accessibility.
- Research current accessibility features in popular devices like smartphones and tablets (e.g., screen readers, voice commands) and propose enhancements.
- Design a feature for the tablet that would specifically help users with one type of disability (e.g., a voice assistant for visually impaired users).

2.12 Fun Activity

WORD SEARCH

INSTRUCTIONS

Find nine expressions related to Artificial Intelligence.
The expressions will appear either vertically or horizontally within the puzzle.

C	W	R	T	I	O	P	S	V	A	R	B	N	O	E
J	L	R	C	E	P	T	P	Y	U	I	S	B	F	H
M	A	C	H	I	N	E	L	E	A	R	N	I	N	G
U	K	Z	A	S	E	Y	F	C	O	X	E	G	O	E
R	A	U	T	G	U	L	M	K	W	L	N	D	D	K
O	V	L	B	C	R	O	U	N	I	B	U	A	P	C
B	R	F	O	I	A	V	T	N	L	P	G	T	C	T
O	H	O	T	H	L	P	R	D	L	V	Y	A	K	P
T	B	K	T	D	N	J	O	J	D	E	S	O	F	J
I	N	P	D	E	E	P	L	E	A	R	N	I	N	G
C	O	I	R	X	T	A	L	N	L	S	Z	A	B	T
S	I	T	F	A	W	M	U	T	P	S	T	H	I	I
Y	V	L	H	E	O	I	C	B	P	J	K	I	O	O
P	A	L	G	O	R	I	T	H	M	D	R	L	T	T
J	O	I	L	I	K	F	R	C	Y	S	U	A	G	K

NEED HELP?
Use the definitions on the following page to help you.
There are two expressions which are acronyms.

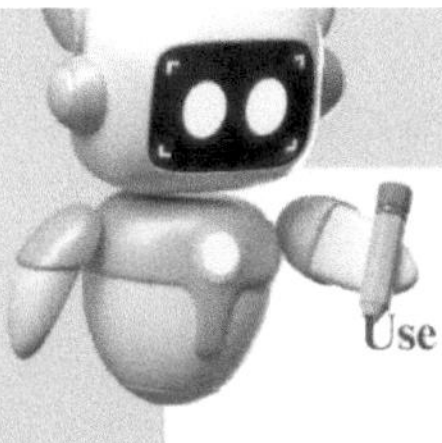

CLUES

Use these definitions to help you find the expressions in the grid. Remember that there are two expressions which are acronyms.

1. The ability of computers to understand and produce language almost in the same way that humans can. (ACRONYM)
2. A computing system inspired by the structure of the human brain used to teach machines to recognise patterns and make predictions.
3. A set of commands that a computer follows to solve a specific problem or task.
4. A branch of engineering that deals with the development and use of robots to perform human tasks.
5. Devices, vehicles, buildings, and other physical objects equipped with sensors, software, and connectivity to exchange data. (ACRONYM)
6. A subset of machine learning consisting of neural networks with multiple layers.
7. A software application designed to hold a conversation with human users.
8. The ability of a computer system to learn and improve from experience.
9. Data sets that are too large or complex for traditional databases.

Students' Discussion on Human-Machine Interaction

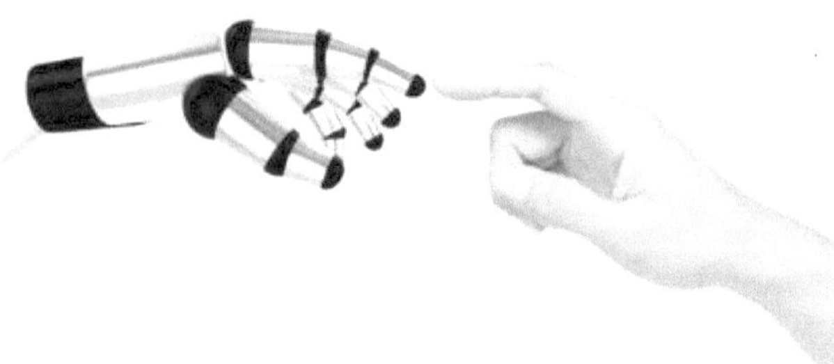

Chapter-2
Test Paper
Human-Machine Interaction

Time Duration: 40 Minutes **Maximum Marks: 30**

General Instructions:
1. This paper consists of twelve questions and is divided into two sections: A and B.
2. All questions are compulsory.
3. Section A comprises MCQs, Fill in the blanks, True or False, and One word of one mark each.
4. Section B comprises answering the following questions with three marks each.

SECTION-A

I - Choose the correct answer from the given options. **(1 X 2 = 2 marks)**

1. Human-Machine Interaction (HMI) primarily focuses on:
   a) Data transmission
   b) Communication between humans and machines
   c) Software design
   d) Physical hardware development

2. Which of the following is not a component of HMI?
   a) Input
   b) Processing
   c) Feedback
   d) Manual overrides

II - Fill in the blank space with the correct word. **(1 X 2 = 2 marks)**

1. The interaction between humans and machines is called ____________.
2. The __________________stage involves the machine processing the input given by the user.

III - Check if the sentence is true or false. **(1 X 2 = 2 marks)**

1. Graphical User Interface (GUI) uses text commands.
2. Brain-Computer Interface (BCI) requires physical contact to function.

IV Write the answer in one word. **(1 X 2 = 2 marks)**

1. What technology overlays digital elements in the real world?
2. What system allows communication between the brain and devices?

SECTION-B

V - Answer the following questions in your own words. **(3 X 4 = 12 marks)**

1. Explain the significance of the feedback stage in Human-Machine Interaction.
2. What are the main components of HMI, and why are they important?
3. Describe the evolution of Human-Machine Interaction from early systems to modern ones.
4. How do voice assistants enhance Human-Machine Interaction?

Answer

Exercise 1- 1. b) **2.** c) **3.** b) **4.** b) **5.** c)
Exercise 2- 1. True **2.** False **3.** True **4.** False **5.** True
Exercise 3- 1. Human-Machine Interaction **2.** BCI (Brain-Computer Interface) **3.** Voice **4.** Touch **5.** Emotional
Exercise 4- 1. c. **2.** a. **3.** b) **4.** d. **5.** e.

Online Resources

Online Exam Paper Link:
Link: https://forms.gle/9ULzP4MJnb584y5t9
QR Code:

Chapter 2 Videos Link:
Link: https://www.youtube.com/playlist?list=PLzlh_31VWEFrAsnGJGRHGgslk2ez6Mnqq
QR Code:

More Sample Test Paper

Chapter 2 Test Paper – 1 Link:
Link: https://forms.gle/VHvcuvXtU9d2QHKD6
QR Code:

Chapter 2 Test Paper – 2 Link:
Link: https://forms.gle/fPiPn3JnrTfEcZrB7
QR Code:

Chapter 2 Test Paper – 3 Link:
Link: https://forms.gle/u19eMohAwW7DSfda9
QR Code:

Chapter 2 Test Paper – 4 Link:
Link: https://forms.gle/2WzLmKJ8oTFqqBgt5
QR Code:

Exam Tips

Manage your time wisely to ensure you attempt all questions.

Chapter 3: Data in AI

Learning Objectives

- Role of Data in Artificial Intelligence (AI)
- Types of Data: Structured and Unstructured Data
- Importance of Data in AI: Training, Predictions, and Continuous Improvement
- Types of Data Analytics: Descriptive, Diagnostic, Predictive, Prescriptive
- Data Visualization Tools: Tableau, Google Data Studio, Microsoft Power BI, Matplotlib
- Data Visualization Techniques: Bar Charts, Line Charts, Scatter Plots, Heat Maps, Pie Charts, Histograms

In the digital world we live in, Data is everywhere. Whether it's browsing the internet, using social media, watching videos, or shopping online, every activity generates Data. This Data is the foundation that powers Artificial Intelligence (AI) systems, enabling them to learn, make decisions, and improve over time. Data is often referred to as the "fuel" of AI, and understanding how AI uses Data is essential for understanding how modern technology functions.

3.1 What is Data?

Data refers to any collection of facts, figures, or information that can be used for analysis. Data can take many forms, including numbers, text, images, videos, and sounds. Data is any raw information that can be processed and analysed to generate useful insights.

For example:

When you type a search query into Google, the words you type are considered Data.
When you post a picture on Instagram, the image becomes Data.
When a store records the number of products sold daily, that record is also Data.
Data can be structured or unstructured and come from various sources, such as sensors, user interactions, or online Databases.

3.2 Importance of Data in AI

Data is essential in AI because AI systems rely on Data to learn and perform tasks. Without Data, AI would not be able to function effectively. Just like humans use experience and knowledge to make decisions, AI systems need vast amounts of Data to learn from.

Here are some reasons why Data is so crucial in AI:

3.2.1 Training AI models

AI models need Data to train themselves. During training, AI systems analyse large amounts of Data to identify patterns and relationships. For example, if you wanted to train an AI system to recognise animals in photos, you would feed it thousands of labeled images of different animals. The more Data the AI system is trained on, the better it becomes at recognising those animals in new images.

3.2.2 Making predictions

AI systems use Data to predict future outcomes. For example, a Netflix recommendation system uses Data about your viewing habits to predict which shows or movies you want to watch next. These predictions are made by analysing patterns in your past behaviour and comparing them with the behaviour of other users.

3.2.3 Continuous improvement

AI systems are designed to improve over time as they are exposed to more Data. For instance, voice assistants like Siri or Google Assistant become better at understanding speech as they process more interactions with different users. This process, called continuous learning, allows AI systems to adapt and refine their performance as they gather more Data.

3.2.4 Solving complex problems

AI systems can quickly analyse massive Datasets, making them especially useful for solving complex problems. For example, in Healthcare, AI systems can process large amounts of Medical Data to help doctors diagnose diseases more accurately. Similarly, AI systems can analyse environmental Data to predict natural disasters or help businesses make informed decisions based on market trends.

3.3 Data types and Data sources

AI systems work with different types of Data from various sources. Understanding the types of Data and the sources from which Data is collected is critical to building effective AI models.

3.3.1 Types of Data in AI

AI works with two main Data types: Structured and Unstructured.

Structured Data

Structured Data is highly organised and follows a predefined format. It can be easily stored in Tables or Databases and analysed using traditional Data analysis tools.

Examples of Structured Data include:

A spreadsheet containing a list of products and their prices.

A Database with customer information, such as names, addresses, and phone numbers.

Product	Price
1. The Jungle Adventure book	250
2. Notebook	60
3. Pencil box	50
4. School bag	700
5. Water bottle	350

Use in AI:

Structured Data is commonly used in predictive analytics and Machine Learning models that require clean, labeled Data to learn from.

Unstructured Data

Unstructured Data does not follow a specific format, making it more challenging to analyse. It includes things like text, images, audio, and videos.

Examples of Unstructured Data include:

Social media posts, emails, and blog articles.
Images and videos uploaded to platforms like Instagram or YouTube.
Audio recordings from voice assistants or customer service calls.

Use in AI:

Unstructured Data is used in AI applications such as Natural Language Processing (NLP) and Computer Vision. For instance, AI systems can analyse customer reviews to determine the general sentiment or use image recognition algorithms to identify objects in photos.

3.3.2 Data Sources in AI

Data used in AI comes from various sources, each providing valuable information that AI systems can analyse and learn from.

Sensor Data

Sensors are devices that gather real-time Data from the environment. For example, self-driving cars use sensors to collect Data on the car's surroundings, such as nearby vehicles, pedestrians, and road conditions. This Data is crucial for making driving decisions like when to turn, stop, or accelerate.

User-Generated Data

User-generated Data comes from users interacting with online platforms or digital devices. This includes:

Search queries on Google

Social media posts, likes, and comments.
Purchase history on e-commerce sites like Amazon.
User-generated Data is valuable for personalising experiences, such as suggesting relevant products or content based on past behaviour.

Open Data

Open Data is freely available information provided by governments, organisations, or other entities. Examples include Weather Data, Traffic Data, and Public Health Statistics. Open Data is often used in AI models to make predictions, such as forecasting weather conditions or traffic patterns.

Proprietary Data

Proprietary Data is privately owned by a company or organisation and is not publicly available. Companies use proprietary Data, such as customer purchase histories or internal reports, to build AI models that give them a competitive advantage.

3.4 Introduction to Data Analytics

Data Analytics examines Datasets to discover trends, patterns, and insights. AI systems rely heavily on Data Analytics to transform raw Data into helpful information for learning, predictions, and decision-making.

Types of Data Analytics

There are different types of Data Analytics, each serving a unique purpose:

Descriptive Analytics

Descriptive Analytics helps summarise and explain past Data. It answers "What happened?" by providing a snapshot of past events. For example, a business might use descriptive analytics to determine how many products were sold last month.

Diagnostic Analytics
Diagnostic Analytics goes deeper to answer the question, "Why did something happen?" It involves analysing Data to understand the causes behind a specific outcome. For example, if a company's sales drop, diagnostic analytics might reveal that a new competitor entered the market, causing a decrease in sales.

Predictive Analytics
Predictive Analytics uses past Data to predict future events. For instance, AI systems might use predictive analytics to forecast future stock prices or predict customer behaviour based on past interactions.

Prescriptive Analytics
Prescriptive Analytics predicts future outcomes and recommends actions to achieve desired results. For example, if predictive analytics shows a decline in sales, prescriptive analytics might recommend adjusting marketing strategies or offering discounts to increase future sales.

3.5 Data Visualization Tools and Techniques
Data visualisation is turning Data into visual representations like charts, graphs, and maps to make it easier to understand. In AI, Data Visualisation helps users interpret the results of Data Analysis and make informed decisions.

3.5.1 Why Data Visualization is important
Vast amounts of Data can be overwhelming and challenging to understand. Data visualisation simplifies this by presenting the Data in an easy-to-interpret format. It helps highlight key trends, patterns, and relationships.

For example:
A line chart shows how a company's revenue has changed.
A bar
chart can compare the sales of different products.
A heat map can display the distribution of Data across geographic regions.
Data visualisation lets users quickly grasp essential information and decide based on those insights.

3.5.2 Popular Data Visualization Tools

Tableau:
Tableau is a powerful tool for creating interactive Dashboards and Data Visualisations. It is widely used in Business Analytics to display Data visually appealingly and easily.

Drag-and-drop interface for ease of use
Customisable dashboards
Integration with multiple Data sources (Excel, Oracle, etc.)
Real-time Data updates

Google Data Studio:
Google Data Studio is a free tool for creating custom reports and visualisations. It is often used for Digital Marketing and Performance Analysis.

Free integration with Google products (Analytics, Ads)
Real-time collaboration and sharing
Customisable templates and reports
Cloud-based, with automatic Data updates

Microsoft Power BI:

Power BI is another popular tool for creating real-time visual reports. It integrates well with other Microsoft applications and is used in Business Intelligence.

AI-driven analytics and visualisations
Real-time Data insights
Integration with Microsoft Excel and other tools
Easy sharing and collaboration options

Matplotlib (Python):

Matplotlib is a Python library used by Data Scientists to create a variety of static, animated, and interactive visualisations. It is commonly used in AI research and Data Science projects.

Wide range of chart types (Line, Bar, Scatter, etc.)
High customizability for creating complex visuals
Integration with other Python libraries (NumPy, Pandas)
Suitable for AI and machine learning visualisations

3.5.3 Common Data Visualisation Techniques

Data Visualisation is an essential part of understanding AI results. It helps convert raw Data into visual formats, making it easier to understand patterns, trends, and insights. Below are some of the most commonly used Data Visualisation techniques in AI:

Bar charts:

Bar charts are used to compare different categories of Data. They can, for example, show how various products perform in terms of sales.

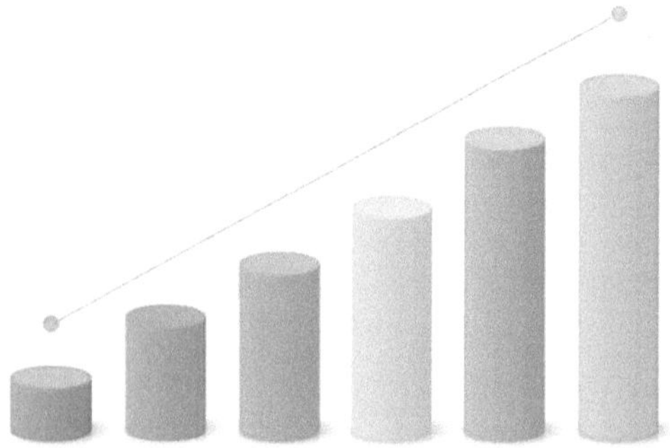

Link: https://youtu.be/7-XO0NFBhXg

QR Code:

Key uses:

Comparing the sales performance of different products.
Displaying survey results, such as favourite sports or activities among students.
Visualising frequency distributions in Data.

Example: A Bar chart that shows the monthly sales figures of four different products, with each bar representing the total sales of one product.

Line charts:

Line charts are ideal for showing trends over time. For instance, a line chart can track changes in revenue over several years.

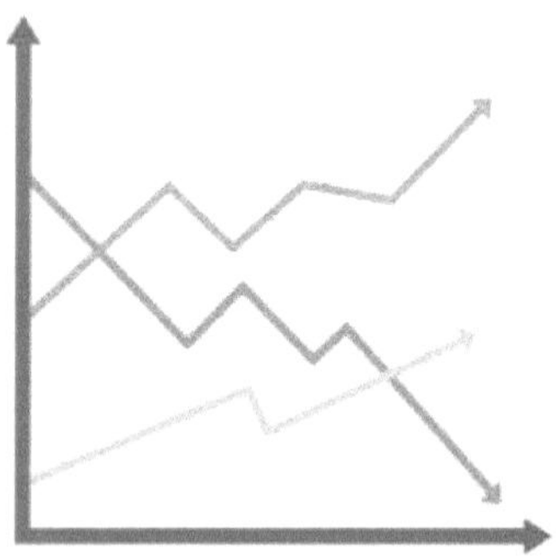

Link: https://youtu.be/sk0BHWSa9jU

QR Code:

Key uses:

Tracking changes in website traffic or social media followers over months.
Visualizing temperature changes throughout the day.
Monitoring trends in market prices or financial performance.

Example: A Line chart showing the growth in the number of active users on a mobile app from January to December, with a steady upward trend visible.

Scatter plots:

Scatter plots are used to show the relationship between two variables. For example, a scatter plot might show the correlation between advertising spending and sales revenue.

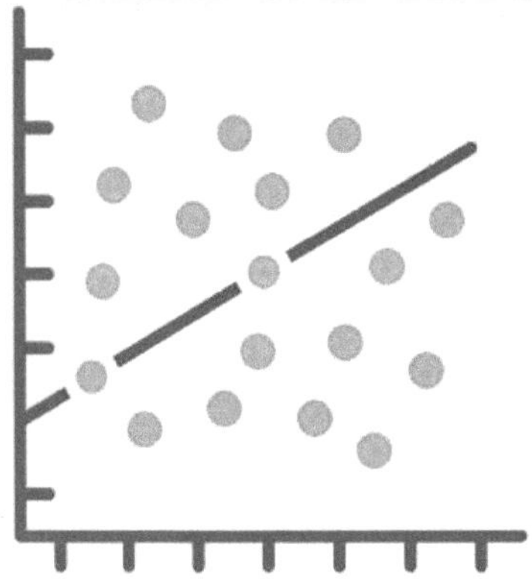

Link: https://youtu.be/2i0xg-Ml1PA

QR Code:

Key uses:

Identifying the relationship between advertising spending and sales revenue.
Examining the connection between the number of study hours and test scores.
Detecting clusters or outliers in Data.

Example: A scatter plot displaying the relationship between a student's study time and exam scores, showing whether more study time leads to higher scores.

Pie charts:

Pie charts display Data as sections of a circle, where each section's size represents its proportion of the whole. This visualisation helps show parts of a whole or percentages, especially when comparing different categories within a Dataset.

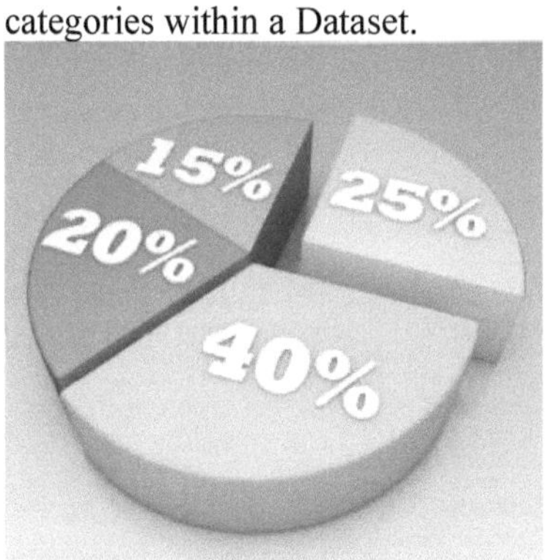

Link: https://youtu.be/VbdXrLPTKD0

QR Code:

Key uses:

Visualising the percentage distribution of different smartphone brands in a market.
Showing the breakdown of a school's budget by different departments (e.g., sports, arts, and academics).
Presenting the share of various social media platforms in total online usage.

Example: A Pie chart showing the percentage distribution of a family's monthly expenses in categories like groceries, rent, utilities, and entertainment.

Heat maps:

Heat maps use colour to represent Data values and help display Data Distributions or identify patterns across geographic regions.

Link: https://youtu.be/RNSAfR5mBfQ

QR Code:

Key uses:

Showing the population density of different regions on a map, with darker areas indicating higher density.

Visualising website user activity by highlighting areas where users click the most.

Displaying temperature variations across a geographical region.

Example: A heat map showing which areas of a city have the most vehicle traffic during peak hours, with red indicating heavy traffic zones.

Histograms:

Histograms display the distribution of Numerical Data. They look similar to Bar charts but show the frequency of Data within certain intervals (bins). Histograms help us understand how Data is distributed over a range, making them valuable for AI when analysing large Datasets.

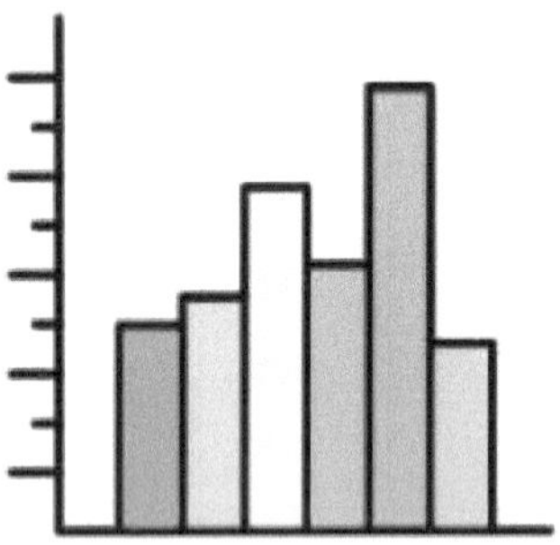

Link: https://youtu.be/yzVZKI1r5Vs

QR Code:

Key uses:

Displaying the distribution of test scores across different students.

Showing the frequency of website visits by duration. (e.g., 0-1 minute, 1-2 minutes, etc.)

Visualising how different age groups are distributed within a population.

Example: A Histogram showing the distribution of students' math scores in a class, with the highest frequency of scores around the average.

3.6 Summary

Data is the foundation for AI, essential for training models and improving their performance.

AI uses Structured and Unstructured Data from various sources, such as sensors, user interactions, and open data.

Data analytics helps transform raw Data into insights through different types (descriptive, diagnostic, predictive, and prescriptive).

Data Visualisation tools such as Tableau and Power BI help create visual representations of Data to improve understanding.

Visualization techniques like Bar charts and Heat maps simplify complex Data, making it easier to identify trends and make decisions.

3.7 Glossary

Data: Collection of facts or information for analysis.
Structured Data: Organized Data that follows a specific format and is easy to store and analyse.
Unstructured Data: Data that doesn't follow a structured format, like text, images, and videos.
Data Analytics: Process of examining Data to discover trends and insights.
Data Visualization: Data representation in visual forms such as charts, graphs, or maps.
Bar chart: A chart that uses rectangular bars to compare Data values.
Scatter plot: A graph that shows the relationship between two variables using dots.
Heat map: A graphical representation of Data depicting values by colour.
Descriptive analytics: Summarizes past Data to explain what happened.
Predictive analytics: Uses Data to forecast future outcomes.

3.6 Exercise

Exercise 1 – Choose the correct answer from the given options.

1. What is the primary role of Data in Artificial Intelligence?
a) To improve the colour of the visuals
b) To power AI systems and enable learning
c) To decrease memory usage in computers
d) To reduce the need for human input

2. Which of the following is an example of Unstructured Data?
a) A spreadsheet with Sales Data
b) A customer database
c) A social media post
d) A table of product prices

3. Which Data Visualisation tool is known for being accessible and integrated with Google products?
a) Tableau
b) Microsoft Power BI
c) Matplotlib
d) Google Data Studio

4. What type of Data Analytics predicts future outcomes?
a) Descriptive Analytics
b) Diagnostic Analytics
c) Predictive Analytics
d) Prescriptive Analytics

5. Which Visualisation technique represents the relationship between two variables?
a) Bar chart
b) Line chart
c) Scatter plot
d) Pie chart

Exercise 2 –Fill the blank space with the correct word.

1. AI systems use Data to identify patterns and make …………………..
2. ………………….. Data follows a predefined format and is easily stored in tables.
3. A ………………… chart helps display trends over time.
4. ………………… Analytics helps summarise past events to explain "What happened?"
5. ……………… use colour gradients to represent Data values and identify patterns.

Exercise 3 – Check if the sentence is true or false.

1. Data Visualisation makes complex Data easier to understand by presenting it in graphical forms.
   ………..
2. Matplotlib is a tool used for Predictive Analytics in AI.
   ………..
3. Unstructured Data can include text, images, and audio.
   ………..
4. A Scatter plot is used to compare different categories of Data.
   ………..
5. Prescriptive Analytics recommends actions to achieve desired outcomes.
   ………..

Exercise 4 – Match each word or phrase in Column A with Column B.

Column A	Column B
1. Structured Data	a) Social media posts
2. Unstructured Data	b) Predict future events
3. Predictive Analytics	c) Organized in tables or Databases
4. Descriptive Analytics	d) Identify patterns in past events
5. Google Data Studio	e) Free tool for creating reports

Exercise 5 – Answer the following questions in your own words (3-4 lines).

1. What is Structured Data?
2. Why is Data essential in AI?
3. What is Predictive Analytics?
4. What are Bar charts used for?
5. What is Google Data Studio?

Exercise 6 - Find examples of Structured and Unstructured Data around you. Write them in a table to understand how Data is present in your daily life.

Instruction

Search for Examples:

Look for examples of Structured and unstructured Data around you — at home, school, or online. Think about the Data you interact with, such as lists, records, social media content, etc.

Write down in the table below.

Structured Data	Unstructured Data

3.7 Project Work

Link: https://www.youtube.com/playlist?list=PLzlh_31VWEFpDrPBxGLCtWnSCaqsabhoY

QR Code:

Attendance Tracker for Student

To create an interactive attendance tracking system in Scratch that allows students to mark and display attendance.

3.8 Group Discussion

Link: https://www.youtube.com/playlist?list=PLzlh_31VWEFo8HsvUnJPP0IXzZCk90MAW

QR Code:

The Role of Data in AI

Discuss the importance of Data in developing AI systems, its impact on various industries, and the ethical considerations involved in Data collection.

3.9 Case Study

Link: https://www.youtube.com/playlist?list=PLzlh_31VWEFpMMfEWIaCfW1cwi8R2YHlZ

QR Code:

Scenario:
A tech company, Tech Smart, is building a recommendation engine for their online shopping platform. The platform collects Data from various sources, such as user search queries, product reviews, and purchase history. The team needs to train the AI model to provide personalised product recommendations based on this Data.

Objective: Students should analyse the importance of Structured and Unstructured Data, and how Data Analytics and Visualisation play a role in training and improving AI systems.

3.10 Fun Activity

Vocabulary Matching

Match the expressions related to Artificial Intelligence with the definitions below.

- [ ] Artificial Intelligence (AI)
- [ ] Neural Network
- [ ] Chatbot
- [ ] Big Data
- [ ] Robotics
- [ ] Machine Learning
- [ ] Natural Language Processing (NLP)
- [ ] Algorithm
- [ ] Deep Learning
- [ ] Internet of Things (IoT)

A) Computers can understand and produce language almost like humans.

B) A computing system inspired by the structure of the human brain used to teach machines to recognise patterns and make predictions.

C) A set of commands that a computer follows to solve a specific problem or perform a task.

D) A branch of engineering deals with developing and using robots to perform human tasks.

C) A set of commands that a computer follows to solve a specific problem or perform a task.

D) A branch of engineering deals with developing and using robots to perform human tasks.

E) Devices, vehicles, buildings, and other physical objects equipped with sensors, software, and connectivity to exchange Data.

F) A subset of Machine Learning consisting of Neural Networks with multiple layers.

G) A software application designed to hold a conversation with human users.

H) The ability of a computer system to learn and improve from experience.

I) The simulation of mental processes done by a machine or computer.

J) Data sets that are too large or complex for traditional databases.

Chapter-3
Test Paper
Data in AI

Time Duration: 40 Minutes **Maximum Marks: 30**

General Instructions:
1. This paper consists of twelve questions and is divided into two sections: A and B.
2. All questions are compulsory.
3. Section A comprises MCQs, Fill in the blanks, True or False, and One word of one mark each.
4. Section B comprises answering the following questions with three marks each.

SECTION-A

I - Choose the correct answer from the given options. **(1 X 2 = 2 marks)**

1. What is Data in the context of AI?
a) A collection of random information
b) A collection of facts used for analysis
c) A physical object
d) A type of hardware

2. Why is Data essential for AI systems?
a) To make AI run faster
b) To enable AI to learn and make decisions
c) To store hardware components
d) To reduce errors in algorithms

II – Fill in the blank space with the correct word. **(1 X 2 = 2 marks)**

1. Structured Data is highly __________ and follows a predefined format.
2. AI systems rely on __________ to learn and make decisions.

III - Check if the sentence is true or false. **(1 X 2 = 2 marks)**

1. Structured Data is difficult to analyse.
2. Unstructured Data includes social media posts and blog articles.

IV - Write the answer in one word. **(1 X 2 = 2 marks)**

1. What is the process of converting raw Data into visual formats called?
2. What type of Data is collected in real-time from the environment?

SECTION-B

V - Answer the following questions in your own words. **(3 X 4 = 12 marks)**

1. What is the difference between Structured and Unstructured Data?
2. Why is Data so important in AI systems?
3. How do AI systems use Sensor Data?
4. What is the role of Data Analytics in AI?

Answer

Exercise 1- 1. b) **2.** c) **3.** d) **4.** c) **5.** c)
Exercise 2- 1. Decisions **2.** Structured **3.** Line **4.** Descriptive **5.** Heat maps
Exercise 3- 1. True **2.** False **3.** True **4.** False **5.** True
Exercise 4- 1. c. **2.** a. **3.** b. **4.** d. **5.** e.

Online Resources

Online Exam Paper Link:
Link: https://forms.gle/zEbUTmg5UHQWwKt37
QR Code:

Chapter 3 Videos Link:
Link: https://www.youtube.com/playlist?list=PLzlh_31VWEFpYufNAsTrmJlvXg4ZtAdK
QR Code:

More Sample Test Paper

Chapter 3 Test Paper – 1 Link:
Link: https://forms.gle/b4hDSxaY48yjxdXu5
QR Code:

Chapter 3 Test Paper – 2 Link:
Link: https://forms.gle/gmAQDd4tADdGSpQZA
QR Code:

Chapter 3 Test Paper – 3 Link:
Link: https://forms.gle/4mQfoCaNcLVKhZf77
QR Code:

Chapter 3 Test Paper – 4 Link:
Link: https://forms.gle/6Bj8dAPvsgFCzZ9LA
QR Code:

Exam Tips

Stay calm and focused – don't let tricky questions stress you out.

HALF-YEARLY TEST PAPER

Time Duration: 90 Minutes **Maximum Marks: 40**

General Instructions:

1. This paper consists of thirty questions and is divided into two sections: A and B.
2. All questions are compulsory.
3. Section A comprises MCQs. Fill in the blanks, True or False, Match the columns, and One-word questions with one mark each.
4. Section B comprises answers to the following questions, each carrying three marks.

SECTION-A

I - Choose the correct answer from the given options. **(1 X 5 = 5 marks)**

1. What is the main goal of Artificial Intelligence (AI)?
a) To create machines that can only store Data
b) To create intelligent machines that can perform human-like tasks
c) To improve the aesthetics of machines
d) To replace all human jobs

2. Which of the following is a component of Human-Machine Interaction?

a) Monitor
b) Algorithm
c) Input devices
d) None of the above

3. Which type of AI is focused on solving specific tasks?
a) Narrow AI
b) General AI
c) Super AI
d) Human AI

4. What is the primary source of Data for AI systems?
a) Hardware
b) User interaction
c) Algorithms
d) Internet speed

5. Which tool is commonly used for Data visualisation in Python?
a) Tableau
b) Matplotlib
c) Excel
d) Google Data Studio

II - Fill the blank space with the correct word. **(1 X 5 = 5 marks)**

1. Narrow AI is designed to perform __________ tasks.
2. AI systems rely heavily on __________ Data to learn and make decisions.
3. A __________ chart is commonly used to visualise trends over time.
4. __________ analytics helps predict future outcomes based on past Data.
5. Human-Machine Interaction begins with __________ devices, such as keyboards and touchscreens.

III - Check if the sentence is true or false. **(1 X 5 = 5 marks)**

1. Super AI is currently used in daily life applications.
2. Descriptive Analytics helps explain why something happened.

3. Input devices are the last stage in Human-Machine Interaction.
4. Data is essential for AI systems to learn and improve over time.
5. A scatter plot is used to display the relationship between two variables.

IV - Match each word or phrase in Column A with Column B. **(1 X 5 = 5 marks)**

Column A	Column B
1. Algorithms	a. Displaying trends over time
2. Narrow AI	b. Brain signals
3. Line Chart	c. Specific task-based AI
4. Brain-Computer Interface	d. Set of instructions
5. Descriptive Analytics	e. Summarizes past Data

V - Write the answer in one word. **(1 X 5 = 5 marks)**

1. Which type of AI aims to surpass Human Intelligence?
2. What is the process of converting raw Data into visual formats called?
3. Which device collects real-time Data from the environment for AI systems?
4. What kind of Data includes social media posts and images?
5. Which Python library is used to create Data Visualisations?

SECTION-B

VI - Answer the following questions in your own words. **(3 X 5 = 15 marks)**

1. What is the difference between Narrow AI and General AI?
2. How does Data play a key role in AI decision-making?
3. What are the main components of Human-Machine Interaction?
4. What is the purpose of predictive analytics in AI?
5. How do Data Visualisation tools help us understand large datasets?

More Online Sample Half-Yearly Test Paper

Half-yearly Test Paper – 1 Link:
Link: https://forms.gle/zLN2pf9MfMnXe4457
QR Code:

Half-yearly Test Paper – 2 Link:
Link: https://forms.gle/dtpw5o13dYDgjNYq5
QR Code:

Half-yearly Test Paper – 3 Link:
Link: https://forms.gle/dXds2yoG6dVXEszw5
QR Code:

Half-yearly Test Paper – 4 Link:
Link: https://forms.gle/SHWysrwFdSP6BxpV9
QR Code:

Exam Tips

Review your answers if time allows to catch any errors.

Chapter 4: Machine Learning Basics

Learning Objectives

Basics of Machine Learning vs. Traditional Programming
Types of Learning: Supervised, Unsupervised, Reinforcement
Importance of Training Data in Machine Learning
Building Simple Models: Image Classifier, Text Analysis
Challenges: Data Bias, Overfitting, Ethics
Real-World Applications: Healthcare, Shopping, Social Media, Assistants
Careers in Machine Learning: Data Scientist, AI Researcher, Robotics Engineer

Machine Learning is an exciting field of Artificial Intelligence (AI) that enables machines to learn from Data and perform tasks that generally require Human Intelligence. Unlike traditional programming, where a human provides explicit instructions, Machine Learning allows computers to "figure out" how to perform a task by recognising patterns in the Data.

Fun Fact: Did You Know?
Netflix uses Machine Learning to recommend shows and movies you might like based on what you've watched before. The more you watch, the better Netflix's recommendations get! That's the magic of Machine Learning!

Machine Learning is everywhere, from your smartphone to the apps you use daily. In this chapter, we'll explore the basics of Machine Learning, how machines learn, the different types of Machine Learning, and how we can build simple Machine Learning models.

4.1 What is Machine Learning?

Machine Learning is a branch of AI that teaches computers to learn from Data instead of being explicitly programmed to perform a task. Think of it like training a pet. When you teach a dog to fetch, you don't program the dog—you guide it through examples and rewards. Similarly, in Machine Learning, the computer learns by looking at many examples and figuring out how to perform the task independently.

Example:
Imagine you want a computer to recognise pictures of cats and dogs. You would give the computer thousands of images labeled as "cat" or "dog." The computer would then analyse the images and learn to identify the features that make a cat different from a dog (like the shape of the ears, the tail, and the animal's size). After this learning process, the machine could correctly label new, unseen images of cats or dogs.

Fun Fact:
The first Machine Learning algorithm dates back to 1959 when Arthur Samuel created a program to help computers learn to play checkers! This simple program became better and better as it played more games, just like a human learning from experience.

4.2 Types of Machine Learning

Three major types of Machine Learning are Supervised Learning, Unsupervised Learning, and Reinforcement Learning. Each type of learning is based on the kind of Data the machine is exposed to and how it uses it to make decisions.

4.2.1 Supervised Learning

In Supervised Learning, the machine is Labeled Data—meaning the Data comes with answers. The machine's task is to learn from these examples and use them to make predictions on new, Unlabeled Data.

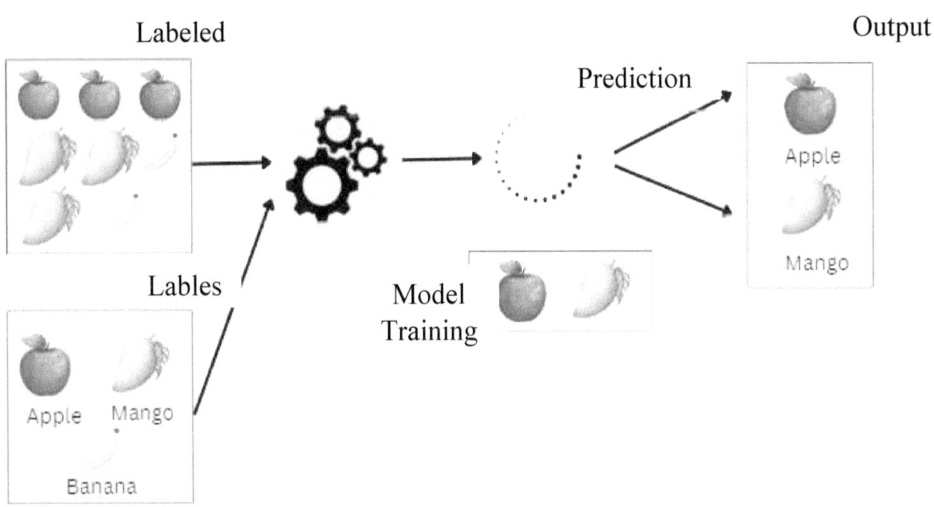

Example:
Let's say we want to train a computer to recognise different fruits. We provide it with a Dataset of images, each labeled as an "apple," "banana," or "orange." The computer analyses the images and learns the patterns that make an apple different from a banana. After training, the computer can look at a new image and accurately predict whether it's an apple, banana, or orange.

Real-life example:
Email services like Gmail use Supervised Learning to detect spam. By analysing thousands of Labeled examples of spam emails, the algorithm learns to identify patterns (like suspicious links or certain keywords) and automatically moves spam emails to your junk folder.

Fun Fact:
Supervised Learning is used in self-driving cars. These cars are trained using thousands of labeled images and videos of roads, traffic signs, and pedestrians. The car learns to drive safely by recognising patterns in this Labeled Data.

4.2.2 Unsupervised Learning

In Unsupervised Learning, the machine is given Unlabeled Data, meaning it has to figure out the patterns and structure by itself. The machine's job is to group or cluster similar Data points without prior knowledge.

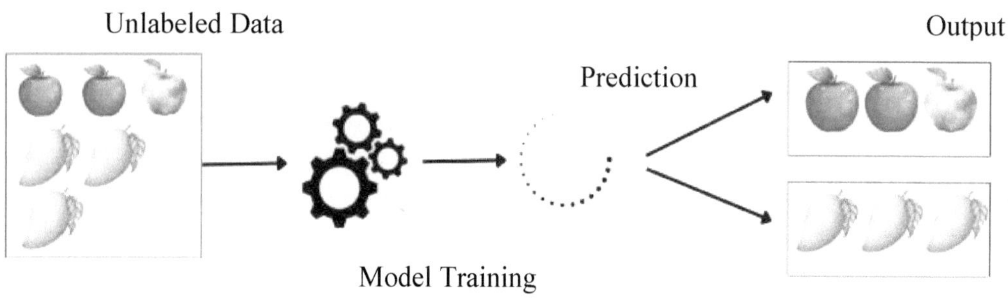

Example:
Imagine you give a computer thousands of images of different animals but don't tell it what kind of animal each one is. The computer groups similar animals based on shared characteristics (like four legs, fur, or wings). The machine might create clusters of similar animals, one group for mammals, one for birds, and so on, even though it doesn't know the names of the animals.

Real-life example:
Unsupervised Learning is often used in customer segmentation. Companies like Amazon analyse customer purchase history to group similar customers together. This helps them suggest products that other customers in the same group have bought.

Fun Fact:
Unsupervised learning is used to create music playlists! Apps like Spotify group songs into categories based on their features (like tempo, genre, and rhythm) and then recommend songs similar to what you usually listen to.

4.2.3 Reinforcement Learning

In Reinforcement Learning, the machine learns by interacting with its environment and receiving feedback. The feedback is given as rewards or punishments, and the machine aims to maximise the rewards over time.

It's Banana | Wrong it's an Apple | Noted! | Reinforced Learning

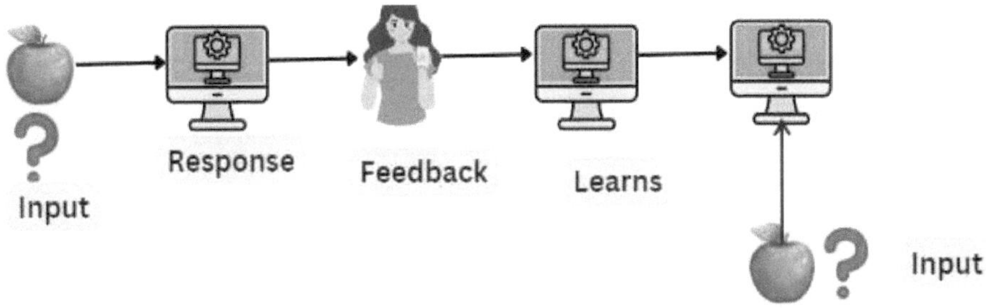

Example:
Think of a video game where you control a character to collect coins and avoid obstacles. If the character collects a coin, it earns points (a reward), but if it hits an obstacle, it loses points (a punishment). Over time, the character learns the best path to maximise rewards.

Real-life example:
Reinforcement Learning is used in Robotics. Robots learn to perform tasks, like assembling products in a factory, by trial and error. They receive feedback in the form of rewards (successful completion of tasks) and penalties (errors or mistakes), allowing them to improve their performance over time.

Fun Fact:
Reinforcement Learning was used to train AlphaGo, a computer program that beat the world champion in the ancient board game Go. AlphaGo learned strategies by playing millions of games and receiving rewards for winning.

4.3 Introduction to Training Data and Models

Training Data is a crucial part of Machine Learning. It is the Data that the machine uses to learn patterns and make predictions. In Supervised Learning, the Training Data consists of Input Data (the examples) and Labels (the correct answers). The machine uses this Data to build a model, a mathematical representation of the problem.

Example:
If you train a machine to recognise flowers, your Training Data would be thousands of labeled images of different types of flowers. The machine would analyse these images to learn the features (like petal shape or colour) that distinguish each type of flower.

Once the model is trained, it can predict new, unseen Data. For instance, you could give the model a new image of a flower, and it would correctly predict which type of flower it is.

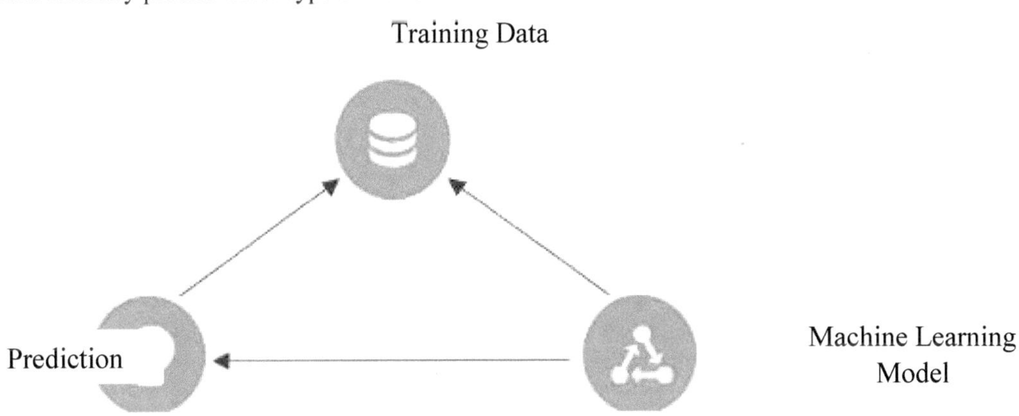

Fun Fact:
The quality of the Training Data is super important. If the Data is incomplete or incorrect, the machine might learn the wrong patterns, just like a student who studies incorrect information before an exam.

4.4 Building simple Machine Learning Models

Now that we've learned about the different types of Machine Learning let's see how we can build some simple Machine Learning Models. Building Models can be fun and educational, and many tools are available that make it easy for beginners.

4.4.1 Building an Image Classifier

An Image Classifier is a Machine Learning model that can categorise images into different groups. For example, we can build a classifier to recognise various types of animals or flowers.

Steps to build an Image Classifier:

Collect Data: Gather images for each category you want to classify. For example, if you're building a flower classifier, collect pictures of roses, lilies, and daisies.

Train the Model: Upload the images and use a tool like Google's Teachable Machine to train the Model. The tool will analyse the photos and learn the patterns that distinguish one type of flower from another.

Test the Model: Test the Model with new images to see how accurately it can classify them.

Improve the Model: If the Model makes mistakes, you can add more Training Data or tweak the settings to improve its performance.

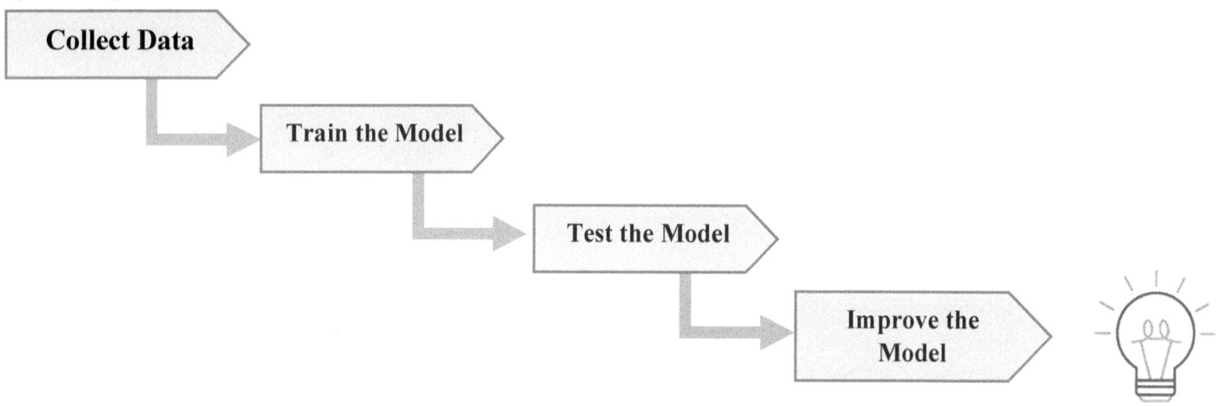

Fun Fact:

Google's Teachable Machine is a free tool that allows anyone to create their Machine Learning models with just a few clicks. You can build models that recognise images, sounds, or even poses!

4.4.2 Building a Text Analysis Model

Text Analysis Models analyse and interpret written language. One common application is sentiment analysis, where the model predicts whether a text expresses a positive or negative sentiment.

Steps to build a text analysis model:

Collect Text Data: Gather Text Data, such as product reviews or social media comments that are labeled with their sentiment (positive, negative, or neutral).
Train the Model: Use a tool like Python or AI platforms that process Text Data. The model learns to recognise the patterns in the text that indicate sentiment.
Test the Model: Test the Model with new Text Data to see if it can accurately predict the sentiment.
Improve the Model: If the predictions are inaccurate, provide more Training Data or adjust the algorithm to improve its performance.

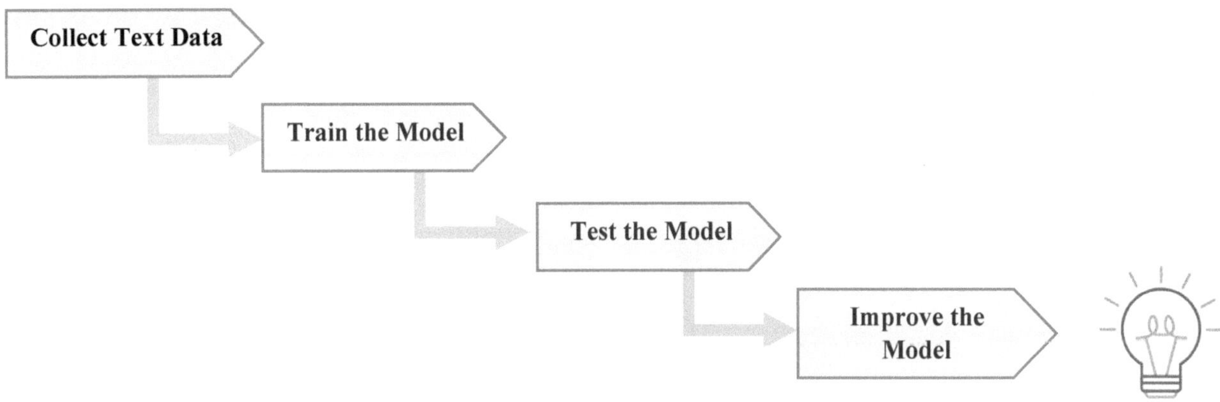

Fun Fact:

Sentiment analysis is used by companies to analyse customer feedback on products. For example, if a customer writes a positive review about a product, the company knows the customer is satisfied. If the review is negative, the company can improve the product.

4.5 Real-World Applications of Machine Learning

Machine Learning has countless applications in the real world. Many things we interact with daily, like social media, online shopping, and even healthcare, rely on Machine Learning to function efficiently.

4.5.1 Healthcare

Machine Learning is used in Healthcare to predict diseases, recommend treatments, and even analyse medical images.

Example:

Doctors use Machine Learning to analyse X-rays and MRI scans to detect illnesses like cancer. The Model can identify patterns in the images that may indicate a tumour or other health conditions, helping doctors make more accurate diagnoses.

4.5.2 Online Shopping

Have you ever noticed that when you shop online, you get product recommendations based on what you've looked at before? That's Machine Learning at work!

Example:
Amazon uses Machine Learning to analyse your past purchases and browsing history to recommend products you might like. The more you shop, the better the system understands your preferences.

4.5.3 Social Media

Platforms like Instagram and TikTok use Machine Learning to personalise your feed. The machine learns from your likes, comments, and viewing habits to show you more content that matches your interests.

Example:
TikTok's algorithm uses Machine Learning to analyse the videos you watch and engage with. It suggests similar content, ensuring you stay entertained and engaged with the platform.

4.5.4 Virtual Assistants

Virtual assistants like Siri, Alexa, and Google Assistant use Machine Learning to understand your voice commands and provide accurate responses.

Example:

When you ask Alexa to "play music," Machine Learning helps it understand your request and select a playlist based on your past listening habits. It can also learn from your preferences to make future recommendations more personalised.

Fun Fact:

In 2019, a Machine Learning algorithm developed by Google outperformed radiologists in detecting lung cancer from CT scans!

4.6 Challenges of Machine Learning

While Machine Learning is powerful, it also comes with its own set of challenges. Machines are imperfect; sometimes, the models can make mistakes or fail to learn correctly from the Data.

4.6.1 Data Quality

The quality of the Data is crucial in Machine Learning. If the Data used to train the machine is biased, incomplete, or incorrect, the machine will learn the wrong patterns.

Example:

Imagine training a machine to recognise cats, but most of the images you provide are of black cats. The machine might struggle to identify cats of other colours because it wasn't exposed to various examples. This is called a Bias in Data.

4.6.2 Overfitting

Overfitting happens when a Machine Learning Model performs very well on the Training Data but doesn't do well on new, unseen Data. It's like memorising answers for a test but failing when the questions are slightly different.

4.6.3 Ethical Considerations

As Machine Learning becomes more widespread, concerns about its ethical implications are growing. Machines may learn to make decisions that can impact people's lives—like in healthcare or criminal justice—so it's essential to ensure they are used responsibly.

Example:

Facial Recognition technology can be compelling but raises concerns about privacy and surveillance. In some cases, Machine Learning models have been shown to perform worse for certain groups of people, which can lead to unfair or biased outcomes.

Fun Fact:

In 2018, an AI system used by Amazon to hire employees was found to be biased against women because it had been trained on resumes mostly from men. The system had to be shut down and retrained with a more balanced Dataset.

4.7 Careers in Machine Learning

As Machine Learning grows, many exciting career opportunities exist for students interested in this field. Companies are looking for people with Data Science, Programming, and AI skills to help them develop more intelligent machines and solve real-world problems.

Careers you could explore:

Data Scientist: A Data Scientist works with large sets of Data and uses Machine Learning to solve problems or make predictions.
AI Researcher: AI researchers explore new ways to develop more innovative machines by improving algorithms and building new models.
Robotics Engineer: Robotics engineers use Machine Learning to build intelligent robots that can perform complex tasks, from assembling cars to exploring space.

Fun Fact:
By 2030, it's estimated that AI and Machine Learning will create over 200000000 new jobs worldwide!

4.8 Summary

Machine Learning is a subfield of AI where machines learn from Data without explicit programming.
There are three types of Machine Learning: Supervised (Labeled Data), Unsupervised (Unlabeled Data), and Reinforcement (Learning through feedback).
Training Data is essential for recognising patterns and making predictions, and Quality Data leads to better outcomes.
Models like Image Classifiers and Text Analysis tools help explore how machines learn from examples.
Machine Learning is applied in healthcare, online shopping, social media, and virtual assistants.
Challenges include Data Quality, Overfitting, and Ethical Concerns as Machine Learning expands.
Career opportunities in Data Science, AI research, and Robotics are growing.

4.9 Glossary

Machine Learning (ML): A branch of AI where machines learn from Data without explicit programming.
Supervised Learning: A type of Machine Learning where the machine is trained using Labeled Data (Data with answers).
Unsupervised Learning: A type of Machine Learning where the machine learns patterns from Unlabeled Data.
Reinforcement Learning: A type of Machine Learning where a machine learns by interacting with its environment and receiving feedback (rewards or penalties).
Training Data: Data used to teach a Machine Learning model. It consists of examples from which the model learns.

Image classifier: A Machine Learning model used to categorise images into predefined groups.
Sentiment analysis: A Text Analysis method that determines whether a text expresses positive, negative, or neutral sentiment.
Ethical considerations: Fairness, privacy, and bias in Machine Learning systems.
Robotics: The field of building and programming robots, often using Machine Learning for complex tasks.

4.10 Exercise

Exercise 1 – Choose the correct answer from the given options.

1. What is Machine Learning?
a) Programming without Data
b) A subfield of AI where machines learn from Data
c) A programming language
d) A type of hardware

2. In Supervised Learning, the machine learns from:
a) Unlabeled Data
b) Random guesses
c) Labeled Data
d) No Data

3. Which of the following is a real-world application of Machine Learning?
a) Making tea
b) Social media recommendations
c) Building houses
d) Manual calculations

4. What happens in Reinforcement Learning?
a) The machine learns through rewards or penalties
b) The machine memorises Data
c) The machine learns from Labeled Data
d) The machine is reprogrammed

5. A common challenge in Machine Learning is:
a) Data bias
b) Collecting hardware
c) Manual programming
d) Writing books

Exercise 2 –Fill the blank space with the correct word.

1. Machine Learning is a subfield of ....
2. In Unsupervised Learning, the machine learns from .... Data.
3. In Supervised Learning, Data provided to the machine is .... with the correct answers.
4. A major challenge in Machine Learning is ensuring the quality of the ....
5. .... Learning involves learning through feedback from the environment.

Exercise 3 – Check if the sentence is true or false.

1. Machine Learning is explicitly programmed for every task. ....
2. Unsupervised Learning uses Labeled Data for training. ....
3. Training Data Quality is essential for better Machine Learning outcomes. ....
4. Machine Learning is used in healthcare to predict diseases. ....

5. Overfitting means a model performs equally well in Training and New Data. ....

Exercise 4 – Match each word or phrase in Column A with Column B.

Column A	Column B
1. Supervised Learning	a) Learning through rewards or penalties
2. Unsupervised Learning	b) Uses Labeled Data
3. Reinforcement Learning	c) Challenges include bias and Data Quality
4. Data Quality	d) Uses Unlabeled Data
5. Applications of Machine Learning	e) Social media recommendations and healthcare

Exercise 5 – Answer the following questions in your own words.

1. What is the role of Training Data in Machine Learning?
2. What is the difference between Supervised and Unsupervised Learning?
3. What is Reinforcement Learning?
4. What are some challenges in Machine Learning?
5. Name two real-world applications of Machine Learning.

4.11 Project Work

Link:https://www.youtube.com/playlist?list=PLzlh_31VWEFrlz9Io3zbyCRIWtmpkE3Wj

QR Code:

Creating an interactive object classifier using Scratch

Students will build an interactive project on Scratch to simulate how an essential Machine Learning object classifier works, using simple programming blocks to recognise and categorise objects.

4.12 Group Discussion

Link:https://www.youtube.com/playlist?list=PLzlh_31VWEFq_WUrcAxtx5z_By3rGf3XG

QR Code:

The Role of Machine Learning in Environmental Protection

Machine Learning is being used to help solve some of the world's biggest environmental challenges. From tracking wildlife populations to predicting natural disasters, Machine Learning models are being applied to gather, analyse, and predict Data that can aid in protecting our planet. In this group discussion, students will explore how Machine Learning can be used to address environmental issues and debate its effectiveness.

4.13 Case Study

Link:https://www.youtube.com/playlist?list=PLzlh_31VWEFo5pzTrFHIfLw-y6bg6e4PS

QR Code:

Using Machine Learning to predict water shortages in a city

A city in a dry region is facing severe water shortages. The government wants to use Machine Learning to predict when and where water shortages are likely to occur so it can manage water resources more effectively. Over the past five years, they have collected Data, including daily water consumption, rainfall, temperature, and population growth. The goal is to create a Machine Learning Model that can help predict and prevent water shortages by analysing these factors.

The tasks need to be performed

Determine which Data (rainfall, population growth, and water usage) is most relevant for predicting water shortages.

Decide whether to use Supervised or Unsupervised Learning and explain why.

Discuss potential challenges (unexpected population growth, weather changes) and how to improve model accuracy.

Consider how the city should use the predictions and ethical concerns to manage public resources like water.

FIND A PAIR

Connect the same elements with a line and circle the elements that do not have a pair.

4.14 Fun Activity

TECH-GEEK BINGO CHALLENGE

Find someone who..

Instructions

Find a classmate for each description. Write their name in the corresponding box. The goal is to fill all nine squares! Get ready to engage, have fun, and achieve "Bingo"! Let's begin!

A branch of computer science focused on creating intelligent machines. ____________	Type of learning where machines learn from labeled data. ____________	A method where the machine learns from labeled data. ____________
Type of learning where the machine groups data without labels. ____________	Data used to teach AI systems to recognize patterns. ____________	Type of learning used by self-driving cars to recognize roads and traffic signs. ____________
The ability of AI to make decisions based on data. ____________	A tool that allows AI to process visual data like images and videos. ____________	A popular AI assistant in smartphones that answers questions. ____________

Chapter- 4

Test Paper
Machine Learning Basics

Time Duration: 40 Minutes **Maximum Marks: 30**

General Instructions:

1. This paper consists of twelve questions and is divided into two sections: A and B.
2. All questions are compulsory.
3. Section A comprises MCQs, Fill in the blanks, True or False, and One word of one mark each.
4. Section B comprises answering the following questions with three marks each.

SECTION-A

I - Choose the correct answer from the given options. **(1 X 2 = 2 marks)**

1. Machine Learning is a subfield of which discipline?
a) Biology
b) Artificial Intelligence
c) Chemistry
d) Physics

2. What does Supervised Learning require?
a) Unlabeled Data
b) Labeled Data
c) Random Data
d) No Data

II - Fill in the blank space with the correct word. **(1 X 2 = 2 marks)**

1. Machine Learning is a subfield of __________.
2. __________ Learning uses Labeled Data for training.

III - Check if the sentence is true or false. **(1 X 2 = 2 marks)**

1. Machine Learning Models learn from Data.
2. Unsupervised Learning uses Labeled Data for training.

IV - Write the answer in one word. **(1 X 2 = 2 marks)**

1. Which learning method uses Labeled Data?
2. What is the critical input for a machine to learn?

SECTION-B

V - Answer the following questions in your own words. **(3 X 4 = 12 marks)**

1. What is Machine Learning, and how does it differ from traditional programming?
2. What is the role of Labeled Data in Supervised Learning?
3. Explain the importance of Training Data in Machine Learning.
4. How does Reinforcement Learning work?

Answer

Exercise 1- 1. b) **2.** c) **3.** b) **4.** a) **5.** a)
Exercise 2- 1. Artificial Intelligence (AI) **2.** Unlabeled **3.** Labeled **4.** Data **5.** Reinforcement Learning
Exercise 3- 1. False **2.** False **3.** True **4.** False **5.** False
Exercise 4 -1. b) 2. d) 3. a) 4. c) 5. e)

Online Resources

Online Exam Paper Link:
Link: https://forms.gle/1ZNqycJngshgJY9B7
QR Code:

Chapter 4 Videos Link:
Link: https://www.youtube.com/playlist?list=PLzlh_31VWEFpUlHKfNj3oPHJGPcZ-a0yf
QR Code:

More Sample Test Paper

Chapter 4 Test Paper – 1 Link:
Link: https://forms.gle/Rw3eBxG5HAMsEEJd6
QR Code:

Chapter 4 Test Paper – 2 Link:
Link: https://forms.gle/KwaVfJss6TbKjo5b8
QR Code:

Chapter 4 Test Paper – 3 Link:
Link: https://forms.gle/Psi1UwSn6T66HPnA9
QR Code:

Chapter 4 Test Paper – 4 Link:
Link: https://forms.gle/nnotft7vQdpyGDGo7
QR Code:

Exam Tips

Get a good night's sleep before the exam to stay sharp and alert.

Chapter 5: Concept of Smart Living

Learning Objectives

Understand the concept of Smart Living and its impact on daily life.
Recognize the role of AI and IoT in enhancing convenience, efficiency, and sustainability.
Identify the key features and functions of Smart Homes and Smart Cities.
Explore the applications of Smart Devices in everyday tasks.
Understand the importance of Energy Efficiency in Smart Living.
Learn about the future possibilities and challenges in Smart Living.

5.1 Introduction to Smart Living

Smart living is about using technology to create a more efficient, convenient, and eco-friendly way of life. The concept revolves around leveraging Artificial Intelligence (AI) and the Internet of Things (IoT) to improve the functioning of homes, cities, and everyday devices. Smart living aims to reduce human effort, cut costs, and enhance comfort by automating simple tasks and optimising resources like energy.

Think about a future where your house can predict your needs, the city adjusts traffic to ease your commute, and your devices handle repetitive tasks for you. Smart living promotes sustainability by using energy-efficient devices and incorporating renewable energy sources like solar panels into daily life. This chapter introduces the growing presence of AI and IoT in our lives and highlights how these technologies shape a new era of living.

How Smart Living works:

Interconnectivity: All smart devices are connected via the internet, which allows them to communicate with each other.

Data Collection: Smart devices constantly collect Data about your habits, such as when you wake up, how you adjust your thermostat, or when you use electricity the most.

Learning: AI analyses this Data and learns from it to predict your future needs or suggest actions, like adjusting the temperature in your home to your preferences.

Example: In a smart home, the AI assistant could wake you up at your preferred time, adjust the room temperature, brew your coffee, and even remind you of your day's schedule—all before you get out of bed.

Fun Fact: The term "Smart City" was first used in the 1990s, but connecting cities through technology has been around much longer!

5.2 Smart Homes

Smart homes are a core part of intelligent living. They use connected devices and AI systems to manage things like lighting, heating, security, and even entertainment. In a smart home, everyday tasks become automated, making life more convenient and energy-efficient. These homes are equipped with sensors and devices that can be controlled remotely by smartphone or voice commands.

5.2.1 How Smart Homes Work?

Smart Lighting: Lights with sensors that detect when someone enters or leaves a room can turn on or off automatically. You can also set timers for lighting based on your daily routine.

Smart Thermostats: These devices learn from your behaviour to adjust the temperature to your liking. For example, the thermostat can cool your home just before you arrive from school, so it's at the perfect temperature when you get in.

Voice-controlled Systems: AI-powered devices like Amazon Alexa, Google Home, or Apple Siri allow you to control appliances, music, and even security cameras with simple voice commands.

Example: You can tell your voice assistant to lock your doors, dim the lights, and start playing a movie while lying on the couch.

Fun Fact: A "smart home" isn't new! The ECHO IV, the first "smart" home system, was created in 1966. Although it never became a commercial product, it could control home temperature and appliances and even create shopping lists!

5.3 Smart Cities

A smart city is an urban area that uses technology to collect Data and manage resources like transportation, energy, and public services more effectively. In a smart city, everything from traffic lights to public waste management is controlled by AI to optimise efficiency and improve the quality of life for its residents. Smart cities focus on reducing pollution, minimising traffic congestion, and enhancing safety.

5.3.1 How do Smart Cities work?

Smart Traffic Systems: AI monitors traffic conditions in real-time and adjusts traffic lights to ease congestion. Some systems can even reroute traffic during accidents or alert drivers to open parking spots.

Environmental Sensors: These sensors monitor air quality and detect pollution levels, helping city planners develop strategies to reduce emissions and improve public health.

Smart Water Systems: Sensors automatically detect water leaks, and smart water meters help reduce waste by tracking water usage in real time.

Example: In Netherlands(Amsterdam), road sensors measure traffic density and adjust streetlights accordingly to reduce congestion. The city also uses smart streetlights that dim when no one is around, saving electricity.

Fun Fact: Dubai aims to become one of the most innovative cities in the world by 2025, with self-driving buses, AI traffic management systems, and even AI-powered public services that reduce waiting times at government offices!

5.4 Smart Devices

Smart Devices are electronic gadgets powered by AI that are connected to the internet. They can gather information, learn from your usage, and even make decisions on their own to improve functionality and user experience. These devices include everything from smartphones and smartwatches to smart appliances like refrigerators and washing machines.

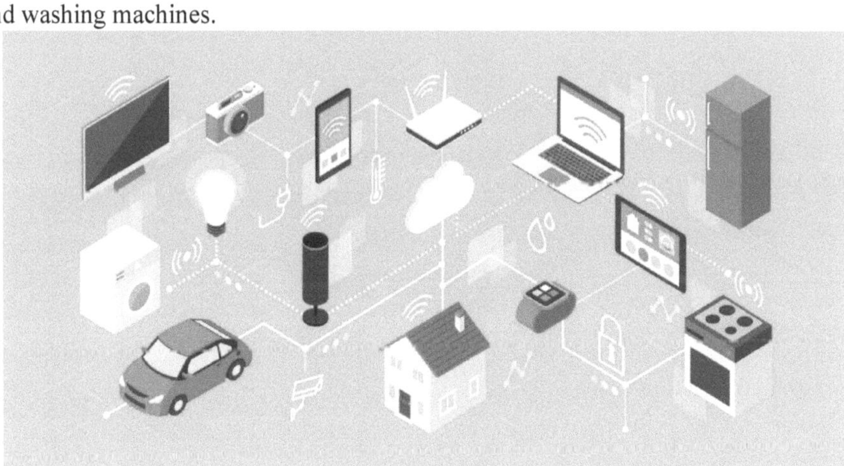

5.4.1 Examples of Smart Devices:

Smartphones: Today's smartphones, like Apple's iPhone or Google Pixel, use AI to recognise faces, suggest apps, and even predict your following action based on usage patterns.
Wearable technology: Devices like Fitbit or Apple Watch monitor your health metrics, such as heart rate, steps taken, and sleep patterns. They also provide personalised insights to help you stay healthy.
Smart appliances: Appliances like smart refrigerators can track the food inside, suggest recipes, and even order groceries when they run low.

Example: An intelligent washing machine can adjust water usage based on the weight of your laundry and send notifications to your phone when the wash cycle is complete.

Fun Fact: Did you know there are intelligent toothbrushes that tell you how well you're brushing your teeth and if you're missing any spots?

5.5 Energy Efficiency

Energy efficiency is a primary focus of intelligent living. It's all about reducing our daily energy by optimising our habits and utilising more thoughtful, efficient devices. Smart devices and homes help reduce energy consumption by automatically adjusting usage based on need.

5.5.1 Energy-Efficient solutions in smart living:

Smart Meters: These devices track real-time energy usage in your home and provide insights on reducing your electricity bill. For example, they can show you how much energy you use during peak hours and suggest alternatives to save money.

Solar Power Integration: Many smart homes are integrating solar panels and renewable energy sources to reduce their reliance on non-renewable resources.

Smart Appliances: Smart refrigerators and washing machines adjust their energy consumption based on real-time usage patterns, making them more efficient than traditional appliances.

Example: A smart thermostat can reduce energy consumption by automatically turning off heating or cooling systems when you leave the house. Over time, it learns your schedule and adjusts accordingly, saving energy and money.

Fun Fact: Studies have shown that using smart devices and home automation systems can reduce energy usage by 10-30% compared to traditional methods.

5.6 Future of Smart Living

The future of intelligent living holds exciting possibilities. With AI, IoT, 5G technology advancements, and quantum computing, smart living will become even more integrated into our daily lives. We can expect even more intelligent systems that make life more convenient, efficient, and sustainable.

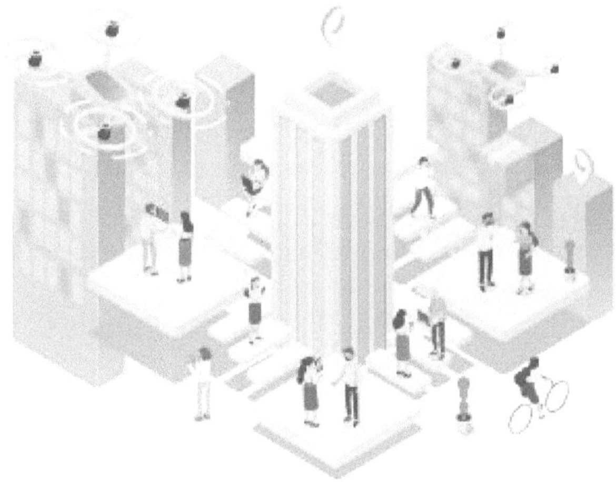

5.6.1 Predictions for the future:

Self-driving cars: AI-powered autonomous vehicles will become standard in smart cities, reducing traffic accidents and improving public transportation systems. Self-driving taxis are already being tested in cities like San Francisco and Dubai.

AI in healthcare: AI will play a more significant role in healthcare, providing real-time patient monitoring, offering personalised treatments, and even diagnosing diseases through advanced AI algorithms.

Sustainability revolution: As more smart homes and cities adopt renewable energy like solar and wind power, the environmental impact of energy consumption will decrease, contributing to a greener planet.

Example: Imagine a future where your car drives to work while you relax or get some extra sleep. Meanwhile, your home runs on solar power, and your refrigerator automatically restocks food when you run out.

5.6.2 Challenges in Future Smart Living: While the future of smart living is promising, there are challenges that need to be addressed:

Data Privacy: As more devices collect Personal Data, ensuring privacy and security becomes critical. Smart living systems must have strict security measures in place to protect users.

Ethical AI use: As AI takes on more decision-making roles in our lives, it's essential to consider the ethical implications, such as the need for transparency and fairness in AI algorithms.

Fun Fact: In the near future, AI-powered drone delivery systems could deliver packages right to your door, and self-cleaning robots could become a common household appliance!

Smart living is revolutionising the way we interact with the world. AI, IoT, and Data-Driven technologies are making our homes, cities, and devices more intelligent, efficient, and eco-friendly. As we embrace smart living, we must also be mindful of challenges like Data Privacy and Energy Sustainability. With these technologies advancing rapidly, the future of smart living promises convenience, safety, and a better quality of life.

5.7 Summary

Smart Living uses AI and IoT for efficient, convenient, and eco-friendly living.
Smart Homes automate tasks like lighting, heating, and security.
Smart Cities optimise traffic, reduce pollution, and enhance public services.
Smart Devices collect Data and improve based on user behaviour.
Focus on energy efficiency through smart meters and renewable energy.
Future advancements include self-driving cars and AI in healthcare.
Key challenges include Data Privacy and Ethical AI use.

5.8 Glossary

Smart Living: Using technology to create a more efficient and eco-friendly lifestyle.
IoT (Internet of Things): Devices connected through the internet to collect and share Data.
Smart home: A home equipped with connected devices that automate tasks.
Smart city: An urban area that uses technology to improve resource management and living conditions.
Smart devices: Electronic devices that use AI to learn and optimise functions.
Energy efficiency: Reducing energy consumption by optimising usage and using smart devices.
Smart meter: A device that tracks energy usage in real-time to suggest ways to reduce consumption.
Sustainability: Using renewable resources and technology to reduce environmental impact.
Data Privacy: The protection of personal information collected by smart devices.

5.9 Exercise

Exercise 1 – Choose the correct answer from the given options.

1. What is the primary focus of Smart Living?
a) Building bigger houses
b) Using technology for efficiency and sustainability
c) Increasing manual work
d) Decreasing internet usage

2. Which technology is commonly used in Smart Homes for controlling devices?
a) Manual switches
b) Voice-controlled systems
c) Cable connections
d) Printed guides

3. What do Smart Cities aim to reduce?
a) Traffic congestion and pollution
b) Number of buildings
c) Internet connections
d) Parks and public spaces

4. Which device can automatically adjust the temperature in a Smart Home?
a) Smart Thermostat
b) Smart TV
c) Smart Fridge
d) Smart Light

5. What challenge is associated with future Smart Living technologies?
a) Lack of AI algorithms
b) Data Privacy and Ethical AI use
c) Too much manual control
d) Overconsumption of renewable energy

Exercise 2 –Fill the blank space with the correct word.

1. Smart Homes use …………………. to control lighting, heating, and appliances.
2. In Smart Cities, AI manages …………….. systems to reduce traffic congestion.
3. Smart devices collect Data to learn from your ……………… and make suggestions.
4. ………………….. Learning involves devices that improve based on feedback from the environment.
5. Energy efficiency in smart living can be achieved through ………………….. meters and renewable energy.

Exercise 3 – Check if the sentence is true or false.

1. Smart Living is only about creating more comfortable homes. ………………
2. AI helps Smart Cities reduce traffic and pollution. ………………
3. Smart Devices cannot learn from user behaviour. ………………
4. Smart Appliances adjust energy usage based on real-time patterns. ………………
5. Data Privacy is not a concern in Smart Living technologies. ………………

Exercise 4 – Match each word or phrase in Column A with Column B.

Column A	Column B
1. Smart Living	a. Automates tasks in homes with AI and IoT
2. Smart Thermostat	b. Adjusts temperature based on user habits
3. Smart City	c. Reduces traffic congestion and improves efficiency
4. Smart Appliances	d. Learns user behaviour to improve functionality
5. Energy Efficiency	e. Focuses on reducing energy consumption

Exercise 5 – Answer the following questions in your own words (3-4 lines).

1. What is Smart Living?
2. How do Smart Homes benefit users?
3. What are Smart Cities designed to achieve?
4. What role do Smart Devices play in Smart Living?
5. Why is energy efficiency important in Smart Living?

5.10 Project Work

Link: https://www.youtube.com/playlist?list=PLzlh_31VWEFqZZDe3h5fjD2B2jo2AwHtw

QR Code:

Create a smart home simulation using Scratch.

Students will use Scratch to design a simple, smart home simulation. The project will demonstrate how various smart devices work together to create an efficient and eco-friendly home.

5.11 Group Discussion

Link: https://www.youtube.com/playlist?list=PLzlh_31VWEFp_edbHSc22mCN6akEqC4xV

QR Code:

The Future of Smart Living

The objective of this group discussion is to encourage students to explore the benefits and challenges of Smart Living. Students will analyse how AI and IoT enhance efficiency and sustainability in homes and cities, discuss potential ethical concerns like Data Privacy, and critically think about real-world applications. By the end, they should have a deeper understanding of Smart Living's impact on daily life and its future potential.

5.12 Case Study

Link: https://www.youtube.com/playlist?list=PLzlh_31VWEFqFUNs2IZO5sa2Ca6SwzmUQ

QR Code:

Smart traffic systems in cities

Scenario: Imagine a mid-sized city that faces severe traffic congestion, especially during peak hours. The city wants to implement an intelligent traffic management system using AI and IoT. This system will automatically adjust traffic lights, provide drivers with real-time updates, and suggest alternative routes to reduce congestion.

Guiding questions for students:

1. What kind of Data would need to be collected to make the traffic system effective?
2. How can AI and IoT work together to predict and adjust traffic conditions in real-time?
3. What role would smart devices like connected cars and sensors play in this system?
4. What potential challenges could arise with this system, and how could they be addressed (e.g., privacy, system failure)?

A Conversation on Smart Living

Oh yeah! I read that Smart Homes have devices like smart thermostats that adjust the temperature automatically based on what you prefer.
It's awesome, but I guess there are some challenges too, like data privacy. All these smart devices collect a lot of information about us.
True. The future of Smart Living will need to find a balance between making life easier and keeping our personal information safe
I agree. But it's exciting to think about where all this technology could take us.
That would make cities a lot more efficient! And I've seen Smart Devices like smart refrigerators that can even order groceries when you're running low.
Yeah, Smart Devices are amazing! They take care of small tasks so we don't have to worry about them

5.13 Fun Activity

CREATIVE THINKING

Create a name for your robot and label it's parts:

____

What is the purpose of this robot?

____

____

____

____

Now assist the robot in completing every maze!

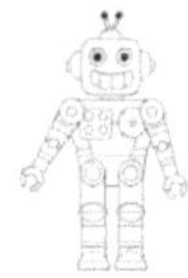

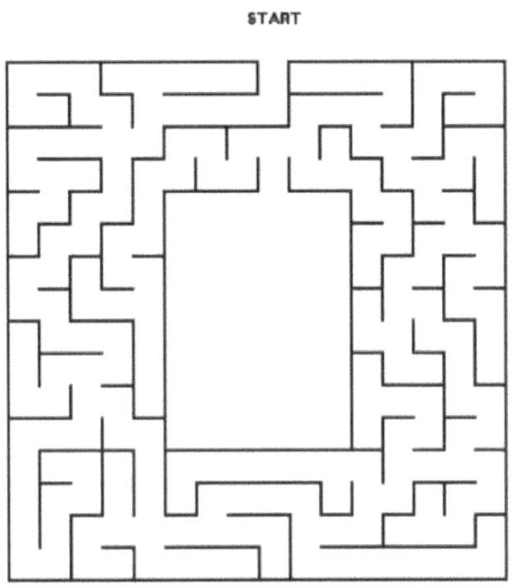

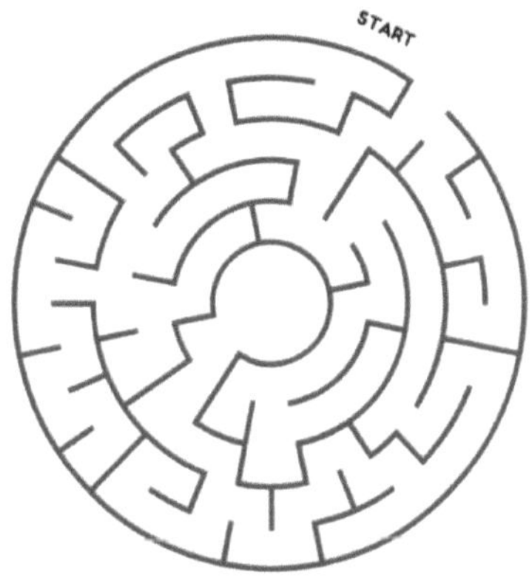

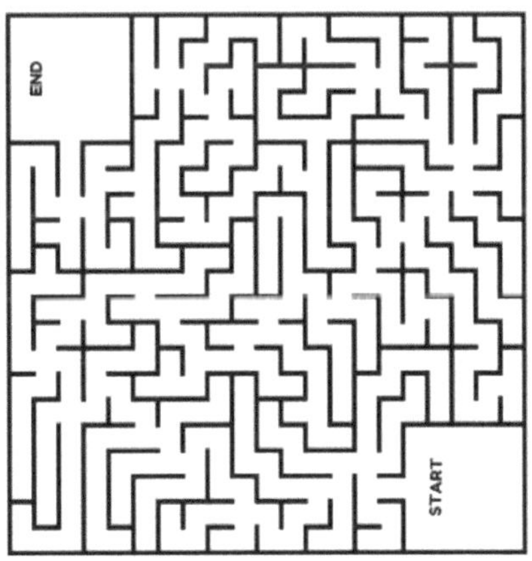

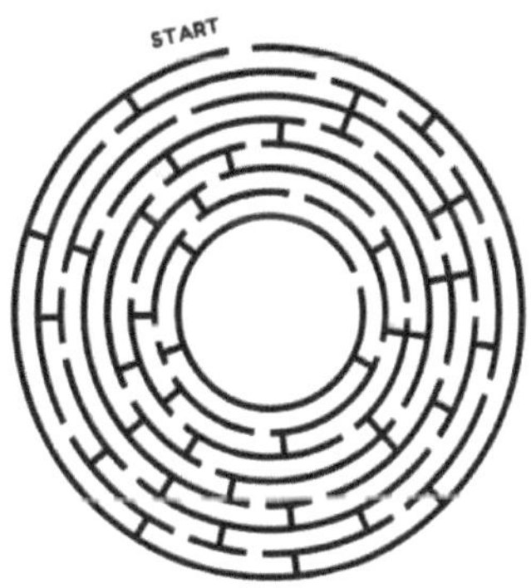

Chapter-5

Test Paper
Concept of Smart Living

Time Duration: 40 Minutes **Maximum Marks: 30**

General Instructions:
1. This paper consists of twelve questions and is divided into two sections: A and B.
2. All questions are compulsory.
3. Section A comprises MCQs, Fill in the blanks, True or False, and One word of one mark each.
4. Section B comprises answering the following questions with three marks each.

SECTION-A

I - Choose the correct answer from the given options. **(1 X 2 = 2 marks)**

1. What is the primary goal of Smart Living?
   a) To reduce technology
   b) To increase manual work
   c) To improve efficiency and sustainability
   d) To make houses larger

2. Which of these is a common feature of Smart Homes?
   a) Automated cleaning robots
   b) Wireless chargers
   c) AI-controlled lighting systems
   c) Manual door locks

II - Fill in the blank space with the correct word. **(1 X 2 = 2 marks)**

1. A Smart City uses __________ to manage resources more effectively.
2. Smart refrigerators can __________ groceries when you are running low.

III - Check if the sentence is true or false. **(1 X 2 = 2 marks)**

1. AI and IoT are essential technologies in Smart Living.
2. Smart Traffic Systems help reduce traffic jams by manually controlling signals.

IV - Write the answer in one word. **(1 X 2 = 2 marks)**

1. What technology connects devices in a smart home?
2. Which device controls home temperature based on user preferences?

SECTION-B

V - Answer the following questions in your own words. **(3 X 4 = 12 marks)**

1. What is Smart Living?
2. How does a Smart Thermostat help save energy?
3. What are Smart Cities designed to achieve?
4. How do Smart Homes use AI assistants?

Answer

Exercise 1- 1. b) **2.** b) **3.** a) **4.** a) **5.** b)
Exercise 2- 1. automation **2.** traffic **3.** behaviour **4.** machine **5.** smart
Exercise 3- 1. false **2.** true **3.** false **4.** true **5.** False
Exercise 4- 1. a. 2. b. 3. c. 4. d. 5. e.

Online Resources

Online Exam Paper Link:
Link: https://forms.gle/w2PViKvfSfh8z39k7
QR Code:

Chapter 5 Videos Link:
Link: https://www.youtube.com/playlist?list=PLzlh_31VWEFplZeDSfw5CT9Dn7oZw2xk-
QR Code:

More Sample Test Paper

Chapter 5 Test Paper – 1 Link:
Link: https://forms.gle/vXe5Ru5vZxZ33uXFA
QR Code:

Chapter 5 Test Paper – 2 Link:
Link: https://forms.gle/F6wZcU1dzQVQunzP6
QR Code:

Chapter 5 Test Paper – 3 Link:
Link: https://forms.gle/dbAuwuxDPcJhfzJh9
QR Code:

Chapter 5 Test Paper – 4 Link:
Link: https://forms.gle/5BZk7R9CfwL6uzVm9
QR Code:

Exam Tips

Practice past papers to get familiar with the exam pattern.

ANNUAL TEST PAPER

Time Duration: 150 Minutes **Maximum Marks: 80**

General Instructions:
1. This question paper consists of forty-four questions divided into four sections: A, B, C and D.
2. All questions are compulsory.
3. Section A comprises two passages carrying five marks each.
4. Section B comprises MCQs, fill-in-the-blanks, true or false, and one word for each mark. The following terms are defined the following terms, carrying two marks each.
5. Section C comprises concise questions with two marks each and short answer-type questions with three marks each.
6. Section D comprises three questions. These are long questions that carry five marks each.

SECTION-A

I - Read the following passage and answer the questions that follow:
Artificial Intelligence (AI) has come a long way since its inception in the 1950s. It started with simple algorithms, but today, AI can perform complex tasks like playing chess, recognising faces, and even driving cars. AI can be divided into three categories: Narrow AI, General AI, and Super AI. Narrow AI focuses on specific tasks like virtual assistants or search engines, while General AI would be capable of performing any intellectual task a human can do. Super AI, which is still theoretical, would surpass human intelligence in every field.

Questions: **(1 X 5 = 5 marks)**

1. What are the three types of AI mentioned in the passage?
2. Which type of AI can perform specific tasks like virtual assistants?
3. Name a task that AI can perform today.
4. In which decade did AI first start developing?
5. Which type of AI surpasses Human Intelligence?

II - Read the following passage and answer the questions that follow:
Smart homes are becoming more popular as people look for ways to make life easier and more energy-efficient. In a smart home, devices such as lights, thermostats, and appliances are connected to the internet and can be controlled remotely. These devices learn from user habits and adjust accordingly, like turning off the lights when no one is in the room or changing the thermostat based on the time of day. Smart homes also help save energy by using smart meters that track real-time electricity usage.

Questions: **(1 X 5 = 5 marks)**

1. What are smart homes designed to achieve?
2. Name two devices commonly found in smart homes.
3. How do smart homes save energy?
4. What is the purpose of a smart meter?
5. How do smart devices learn from user habits?

SECTION-B

III - Choose the correct answer from the given options. **(1 X 5 = 5 marks)**

1. Which type of AI is still theoretical and would surpass Human Intelligence?
a) Narrow AI
b) General AI
c) Super AI
d) None of the above

2. Which component is essential for Human-Machine Interaction?
a) Data Analytics
b) Sensors and interfaces
c) General AI
d) Super AI

3. Which tool helps in visualising Data in AI?
a) Algorithms
b) Data Analytics
c) Visualization Tools
d) Smart Devices

4. What is the key to saving energy in smart homes?
a) Larger appliances
b) Smart meters
c) Manual switches
d) High electricity consumption

5. In Machine Learning, which type of learning uses feedback to improve?
a) Supervised
b) Unsupervised
c) Reinforcement
d) Data learning

IV - Fill in the blank space with the correct word. **(1 X 5 = 5 marks)**

1. ……………….. can perform any intellectual task a human can do.
2. ………………. track real-time electricity usage in homes.
3. ………………………… help in presenting Data for easier understanding.
4. ……………………….. uses Labeled Data to train models in Machine Learning.
5. ………………. use technology to reduce traffic congestion and pollution.

V - Check if the sentence is true or false. **(1 X 5 = 5 marks)**

1. Narrow AI is capable of performing all human tasks.
2. Human-Machine Interaction includes the use of sensors and interfaces.
3. Data Visualisation tools are not necessary for understanding AI-generated Data.
4. Smart Devices in homes can adjust settings based on user behaviour.
5. Supervised Learning in AI does not require Labeled Data.

VI - Write the answer in one word. **(1 X 5 = 5 marks)**

1. Which AI type surpasses Human Intelligence?
2. What tracks electricity usage in real-time in smart homes?
3. What do smart devices collect to adjust their functions?
4. What tool helps visualise complex Data in AI?
5. What adjusts room temperature automatically based on user preferences?

VII – Define the following terms. **(2 X 5 = 10 marks)**

1. Machine Learning
2. Human Machines
3. Smart Devices
4. Supervised Learning
5. Smart Cities

SECTION-C

VIII – Very short answer type questions. **(2 X 5 = 10 marks)**

1. What is Narrow AI?
2. What is the role of Data in AI?
3. How do smart homes use energy efficiently?

4. What is Machine Learning?
5. What are the key components of Human-Machine Interaction?

IX - Short answer type question. **(3 X 5 = 15 marks)**

1. Explain the importance of Data in AI.
2. What are the types of Machine Learning?
3. How do smart homes improve convenience and sustainability?
4. What is the difference between Narrow AI and General AI?
5. How does Reinforcement Learning work in AI?

SECTION-D

X - Long answer type question. **(5 X 3 = 15 marks)**

1. Discuss the evolution of Human-Machine Interaction.
2. How do smart cities use AI and IoT to reduce pollution and traffic congestion?
3. Explain how Data visualisation helps in AI.

More Online Annual Test Papers

Annual Test Paper – 1 Link:
Link: https://forms.gle/HsZn6a38ZSBmpk5G9
QR Code:

Annual Test Paper – 2 Link:
Link: https://forms.gle/Wgxht6ytYudm2vyj7
QR Code:

Annual Test Paper – 3 Link:
Link: https://forms.gle/pH4yatCDsV7gPpWJ6
QR Code:

Annual Test Paper – 4 Link:
Link: https://forms.gle/opjx6UKfo8GDBkkZ7
QR Code:

Tips for Solving Exam Papers

1. **READ THE ENTIRE PAPER**
   Quickly scan the paper to understand the questions and plan your time.

2. **START WITH EASY QUESTIONS**
   Answer the questions you find easiest first to build confidence.

3. **MANAGE YOUR TIME**
   Allocate time to each section and stick to it.

4. **UNDERSTAND THE QUESTION**
   Carefully read each question to ensure you know what's being asked before you answer.

5. **SHOW WORKINGS IN MATH**
   Always show your calculations to earn partial credit if needed.

6. **WRITE NEATLY**
   Present your answers clearly to make them easy to read.

7. **USE DIAGRAMS**
   Include diagrams where relevant, especially in Science.

8. **REVIEW YOUR ANSWERS**
   If time allows, review your answers to check for mistakes.

9. **ATTEMPT ALL QUESTIONS**
   Try to answer every question, even if you're unsure.

10. **STAY CALM**
    Stay relaxed and focused to think more clearly.

Chapter 6: Viva Voce

6.1 Questions and Answers

Question 1. What is Artificial Intelligence (AI)?
Answer: AI is the simulation of Human Intelligence in machines programmed to perform tasks such as problem-solving, decision-making, and pattern recognition.

Question 2. What are the three types of AI?
Answer: The three types of AI are Narrow AI (focused on specific tasks), General AI (capable of performing any intellectual task a human can do), and Super AI (theoretical AI that surpasses Human Intelligence).

Question 3. What is the difference between Narrow AI and General AI?
Answer: Narrow AI is specialised for specific tasks, like virtual assistants, whereas General AI would be able to perform any intellectual task that a human can do.

Question 4. What is Super AI?
Answer: Super AI is a theoretical form of AI that would exceed Human Intelligence in all aspects, including creativity, problem-solving, and decision-making. It has not been achieved yet.

Question 5. How does AI benefit from Machine Learning?
Answer: AI uses Machine Learning to improve its performance by learning from Data and making better decisions or predictions over time without being explicitly programmed for each task.

Question 6. What is Machine Learning?
Answer: Machine Learning is a subset of AI that allows machines to learn from Data and improve their performance without being explicitly programmed.

Question 7. What are the types of Machine Learning?
Answer: The three main types of Machine Learning are Supervised Learning, Unsupervised Learning, and Reinforcement Learning.

Question 8. What is Supervised Learning?
Answer: Supervised Learning is a type of Machine Learning where the model is trained on Labeled Data, which includes input-output pairs, allowing the machine to learn patterns and make predictions.

Question 9. What is Unsupervised Learning?
Answer: In Unsupervised Learning, the model is given Data without Labels and is tasked with finding patterns or relationships within the Data independently.

Question 10. What is Reinforcement Learning?
Answer: Reinforcement Learning is a type of Machine Learning where an agent learns by interacting with its environment and receiving rewards or penalties based on its actions, aiming to maximise cumulative rewards.

Question 11. What is Human-Machine Interaction (HMI)?
Answer: Human-Machine Interaction is the study and design of systems that allow humans to interact with machines, focusing on creating intuitive and efficient interfaces for control and communication.

Question 12. How does AI improve Human-Machine Interaction?
Answer: AI improves Human-Machine Interaction by making interactions more intuitive, such as through voice recognition, natural language processing, and predictive behaviours that respond to user needs.

Question 13. What role do sensors play in Human-Machine Interaction?
Answer: Sensors allow machines to detect and respond to physical environmental inputs, such as motion, temperature, or touch, which is critical for smooth interaction between humans and machines.

Question 14. Why is Data essential in AI?
Answer: Data is essential in AI because it trains algorithms, makes predictions, and continuously improves performance by learning from past information.

Question 15. What are the different types of Data used in AI?
Answer: Common data types in AI include Structured Data (like spreadsheets or databases), Unstructured Data (such as images, videos, or text), and Semi-Structured Data (like XML or JSON files).

Question 16. What is Data Analytics in AI?
Answer: Data Analytics in AI involves analysing Data to extract meaningful insights, identify patterns, and support decision-making. AI models are often used to make better predictions.

Question 17. What tools are used for Data Visualisation in AI?
Answer: Common Data Visualisation tools include Tableau, Power BI, Matplotlib, and Google Charts, which help transform complex Data into easy-to-understand visual formats like graphs and charts.

Question18. What is the role of algorithms in AI?
Answer: Algorithms are the step-by-step instructions AI systems use to process data, recognise patterns, and make decisions or predictions.

Question 19. How does AI contribute to Smart Living?
Answer: AI contributes to Smart Living by automating tasks, optimising energy usage, enhancing convenience in homes and cities, and making systems more efficient, such as smart thermostats or intelligent traffic systems.

Question 20. What is a Smart Home?
Answer: A Smart Home is a home equipped with interconnected devices that use AI and IoT to automate tasks such as lighting, heating, security, and appliance control, often optimising energy usage and enhancing comfort.

6.2 Online Exam Paper

Link: https://forms.gle/rnEhwAqKWQ4EKGLR9
QR Code:

6.3 Online Video

Link: https://www.youtube.com/playlist?list=PLzlh_31VWEFo49x8Jnak7Us8aRAM1S11x
QR Code:

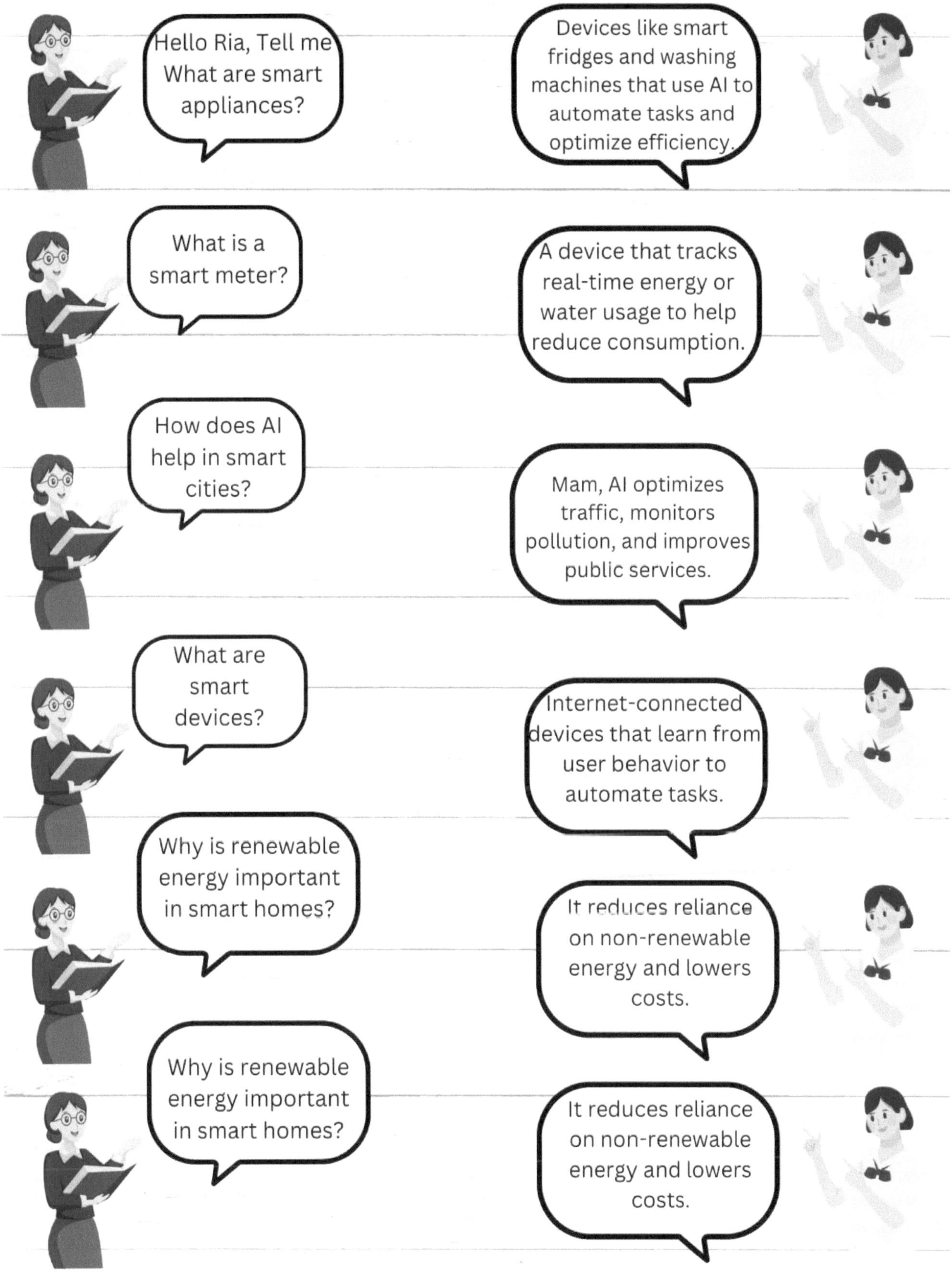
Hello Ria, Tell me What are smart appliances?
Devices like smart fridges and washing machines that use AI to automate tasks and optimize efficiency.
What is a smart meter?
A device that tracks real-time energy or water usage to help reduce consumption.
How does AI help in smart cities?
Mam, AI optimizes traffic, monitors pollution, and improves public services.
What are smart devices?
Internet-connected devices that learn from user behavior to automate tasks.
Why is renewable energy important in smart homes?
It reduces reliance on non-renewable energy and lowers costs.
Why is renewable energy important in smart homes?
It reduces reliance on non-renewable energy and lowers costs.

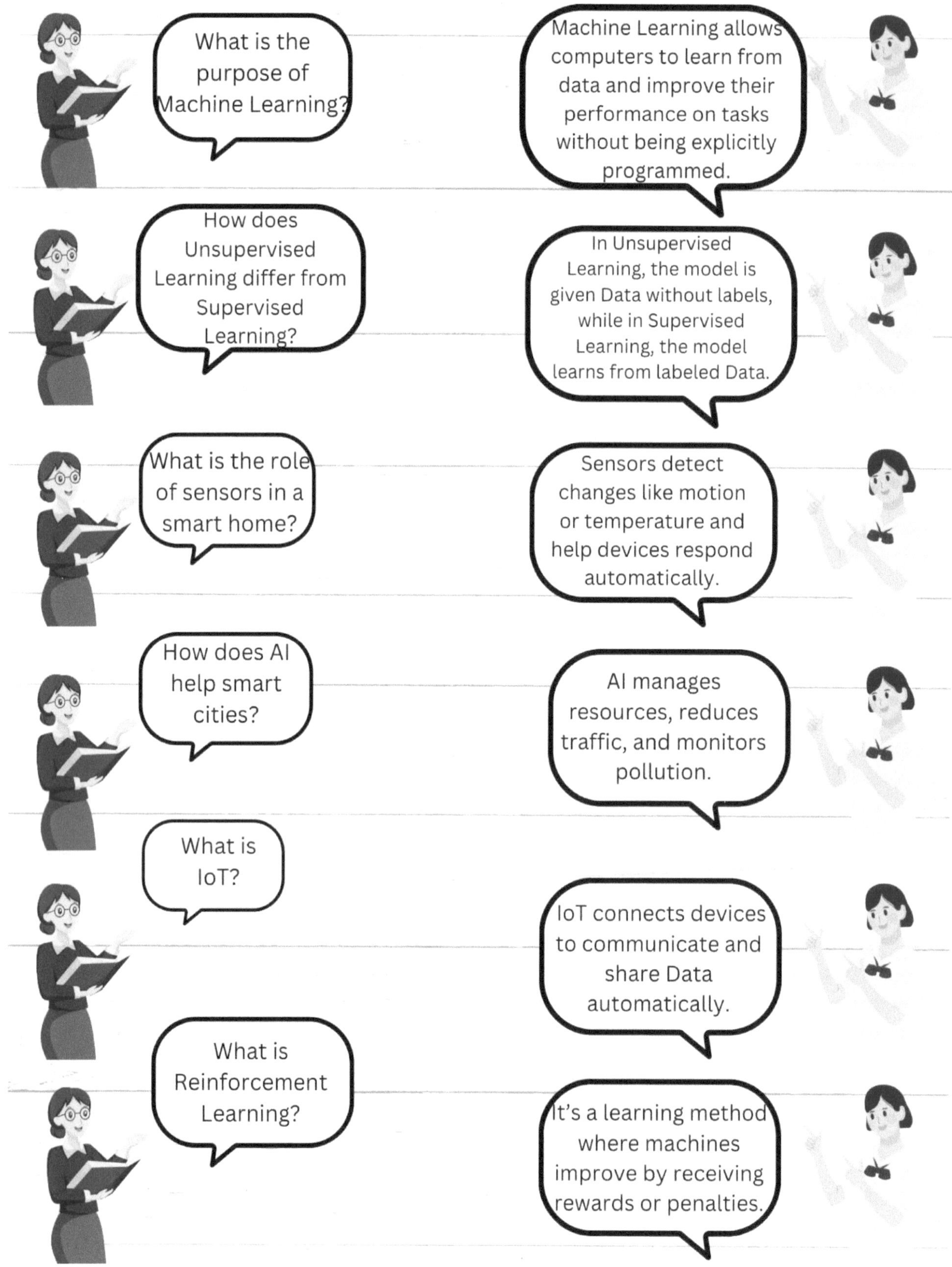
What is the purpose of Machine Learning?
Machine Learning allows computers to learn from data and improve their performance on tasks without being explicitly programmed.
How does Unsupervised Learning differ from Supervised Learning?
In Unsupervised Learning, the model is given Data without labels, while in Supervised Learning, the model learns from labeled Data.
What is the role of sensors in a smart home?
Sensors detect changes like motion or temperature and help devices respond automatically.
How does AI help smart cities?
AI manages resources, reduces traffic, and monitors pollution.
What is IoT?
IoT connects devices to communicate and share Data automatically.
What is Reinforcement Learning?
It's a learning method where machines improve by receiving rewards or penalties.

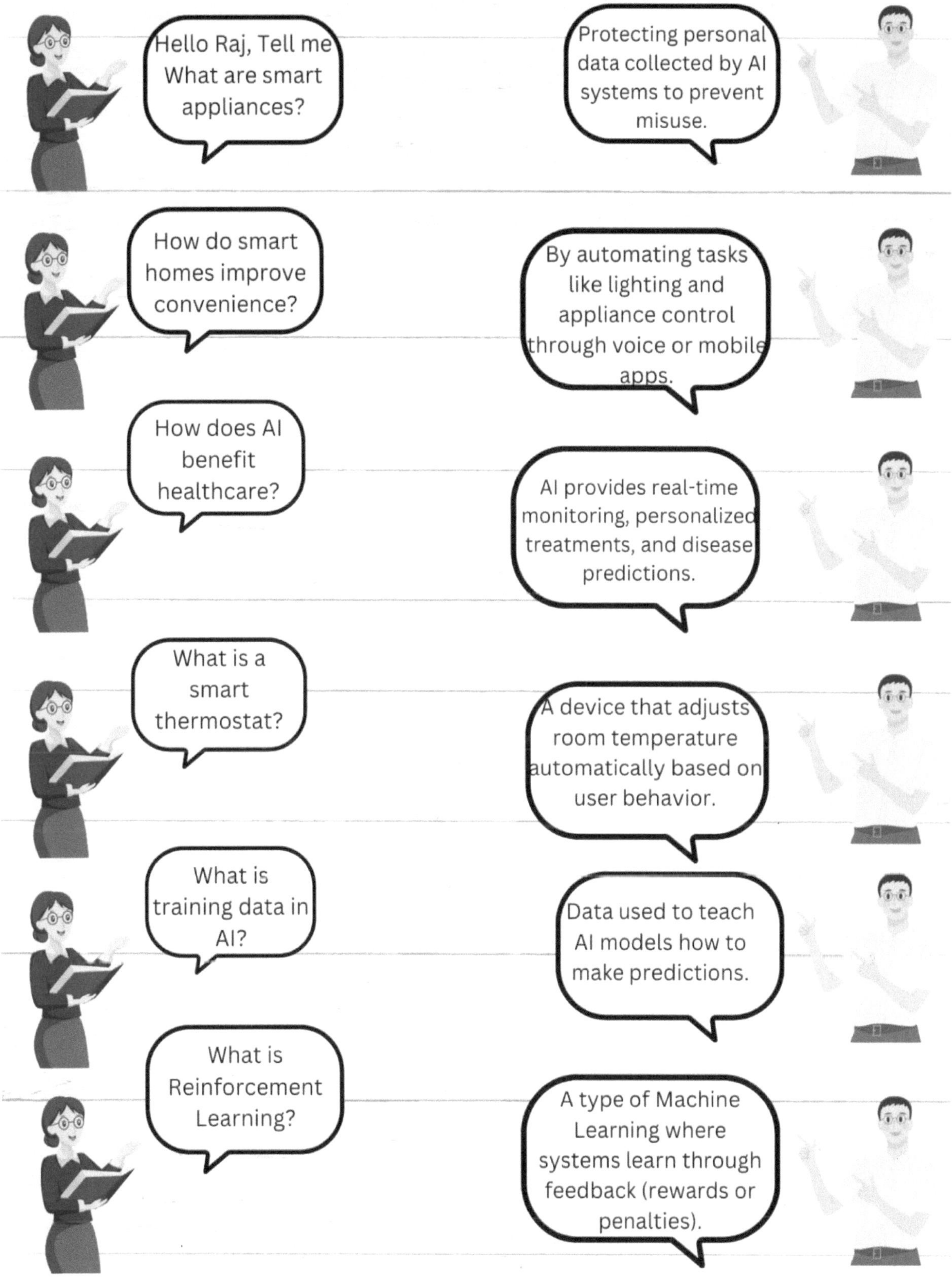
Hello Raj, Tell me What are smart appliances?
Protecting personal data collected by AI systems to prevent misuse.
How do smart homes improve convenience?
By automating tasks like lighting and appliance control through voice or mobile apps.
How does AI benefit healthcare?
AI provides real-time monitoring, personalized treatments, and disease predictions.
What is a smart thermostat?
A device that adjusts room temperature automatically based on user behavior.
What is training data in AI?
Data used to teach AI models how to make predictions.
What is Reinforcement Learning?
A type of Machine Learning where systems learn through feedback (rewards or penalties).

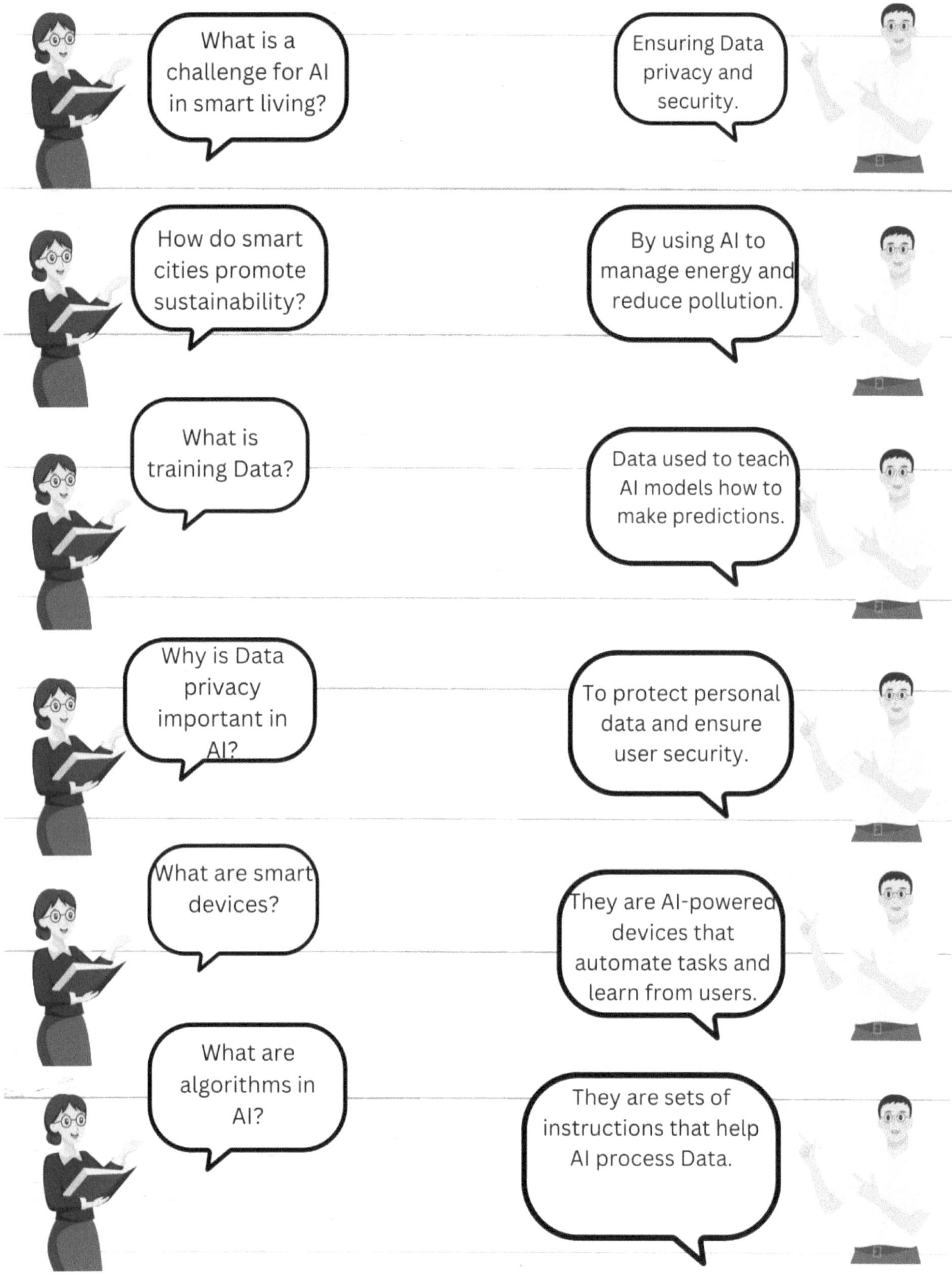
What is a challenge for AI in smart living?
Ensuring Data privacy and security.
How do smart cities promote sustainability?
By using AI to manage energy and reduce pollution.
What is training Data?
Data used to teach AI models how to make predictions.
Why is Data privacy important in AI?
To protect personal data and ensure user security.
What are smart devices?
They are AI-powered devices that automate tasks and learn from users.
What are algorithms in AI?
They are sets of instructions that help AI process Data.

Chapter 7: Introduction to Programming with Scratch

Learning Objectives

Understand the basics of Scratch and its interface.
Learn how to use sprites, blocks, and scripts.
Create simple animations and interactive stories.
Apply loops, conditions, and variables to enhance their projects.

Introduction to Scratch

Scratch is a Block-Based visual programming language designed to make coding easy and fun. It allows users to create stories, games, and animations by dragging and dropping blocks of code. Scratch is especially popular among beginners because it introduces programming concepts without the complexity of typing code.

1. Getting Started with Scratch

Open your web browser and go to **scratch.mit.edu.**

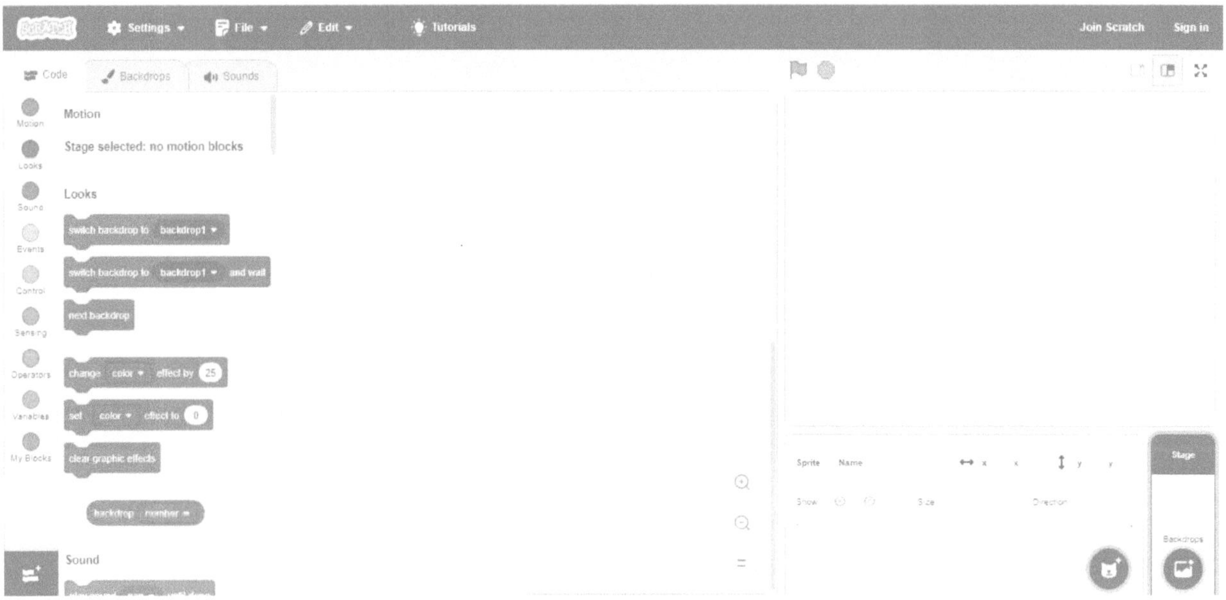

If you don't have an account, create one by clicking Join Scratch. Otherwise, click Sign In.

Once logged in, click Create from the top menu to start a new project.

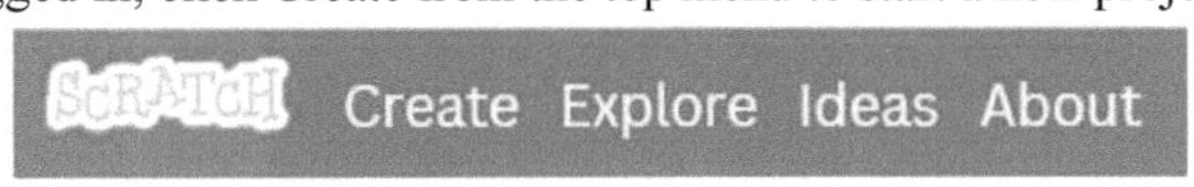

2. Understanding the Scratch Interface

The Scratch interface is divided into several parts:

Stage: Where the sprites (characters) interact and perform actions.
Sprites Pane: Displays the sprites used in your project.

Blocks Palette: Contains all the code blocks you need to program.
Scripts Area: Where you drag and arrange code blocks to create your program.
Backdrop: The background of the stage.

3. Creating Your First Project – An Animated Story

Let's make a simple animated project where a cat and a balloon sprite greet each other.

Step 1: Add Sprites

Delete the default cat sprite by clicking the trash icon next to it.
Add two new sprites: Click the "Choose a Sprite" button. Select Cat and Balloon from the sprite library.

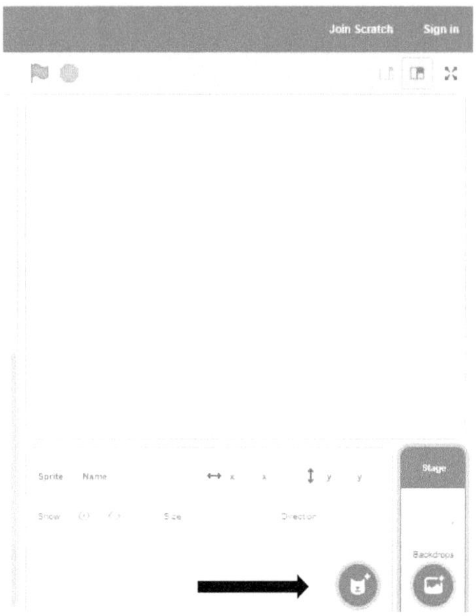

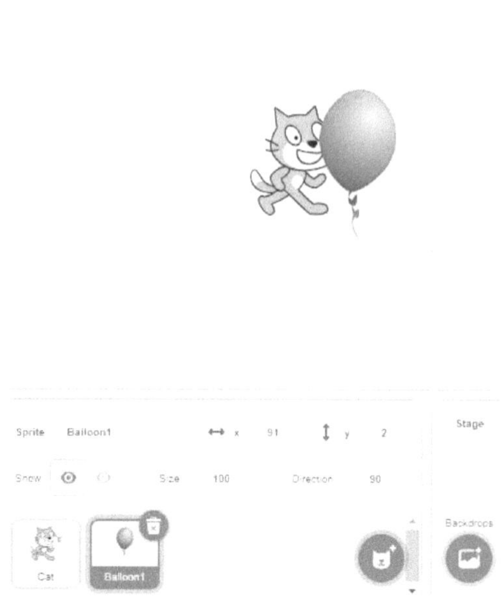

Step 2: Add a Backdrop

Click on the Stage area and select Choose a Backdrop.

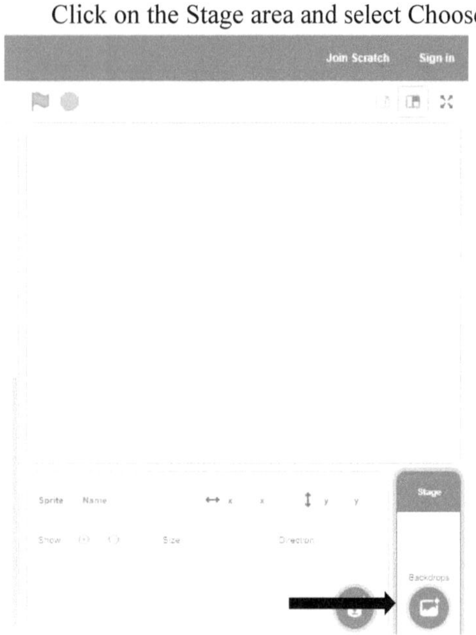

Pick any backdrop, such as Blue Sky, to make your story colorful.

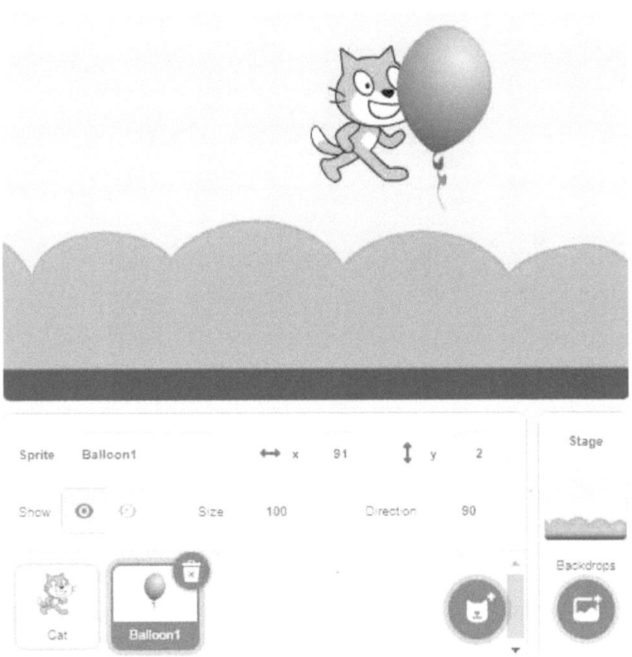

4. Creating Scripts (Adding Code)

a. Script for the Cat Sprite

Click on the Cat sprite.

Go to the Events category and drag the "When green flag clicked" block to the Scripts Area.
Add a "Say [Hello, Balloon!] for 2 seconds" block from the Looks category.
Add a "Move 10 steps" block from the Motion category to make the cat walk toward the balloon.

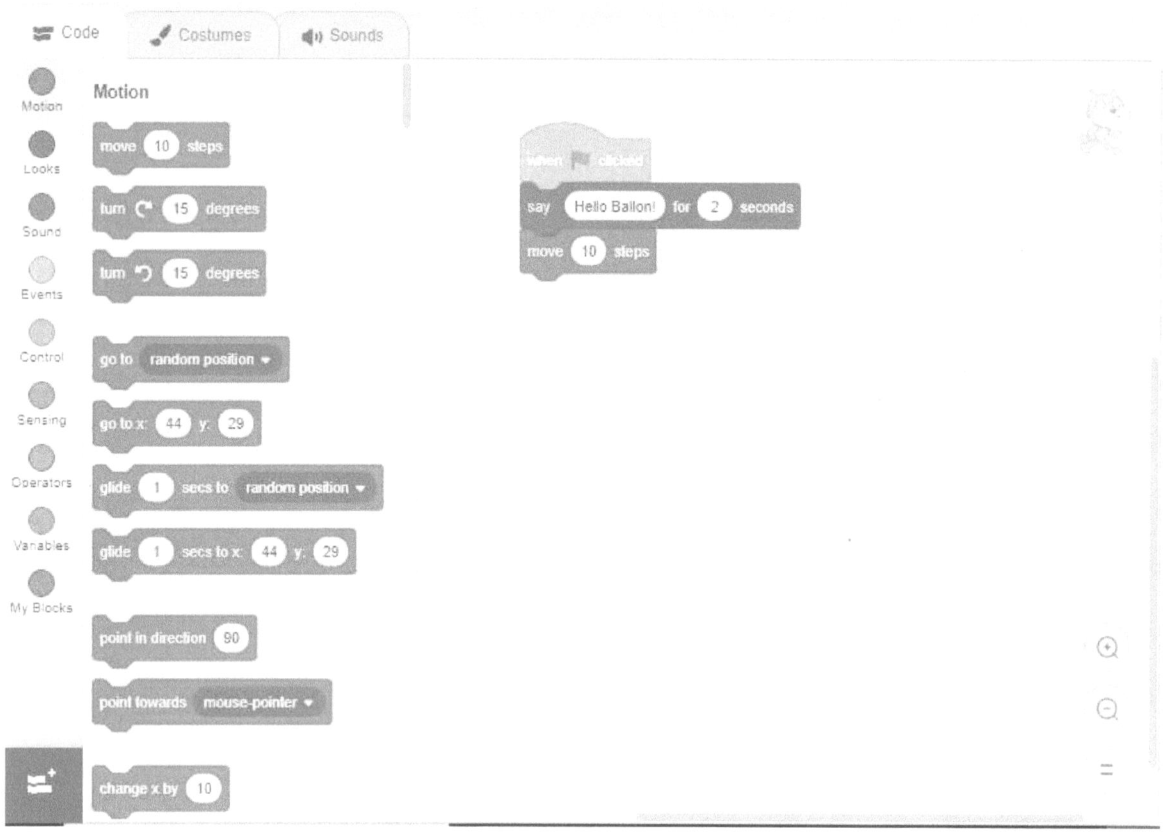

Script for the Balloon Sprite

Click on the Balloon sprite.

Add a "When green flag clicked" block from Events.
Add a "Wait 2 seconds" block from the Control category so the balloon responds after the cat speaks.
Use a "Say [Hello, Cat!] for 2 seconds" block from the Looks category.
Add a "Change size by 10" block from Looks to make the balloon grow.

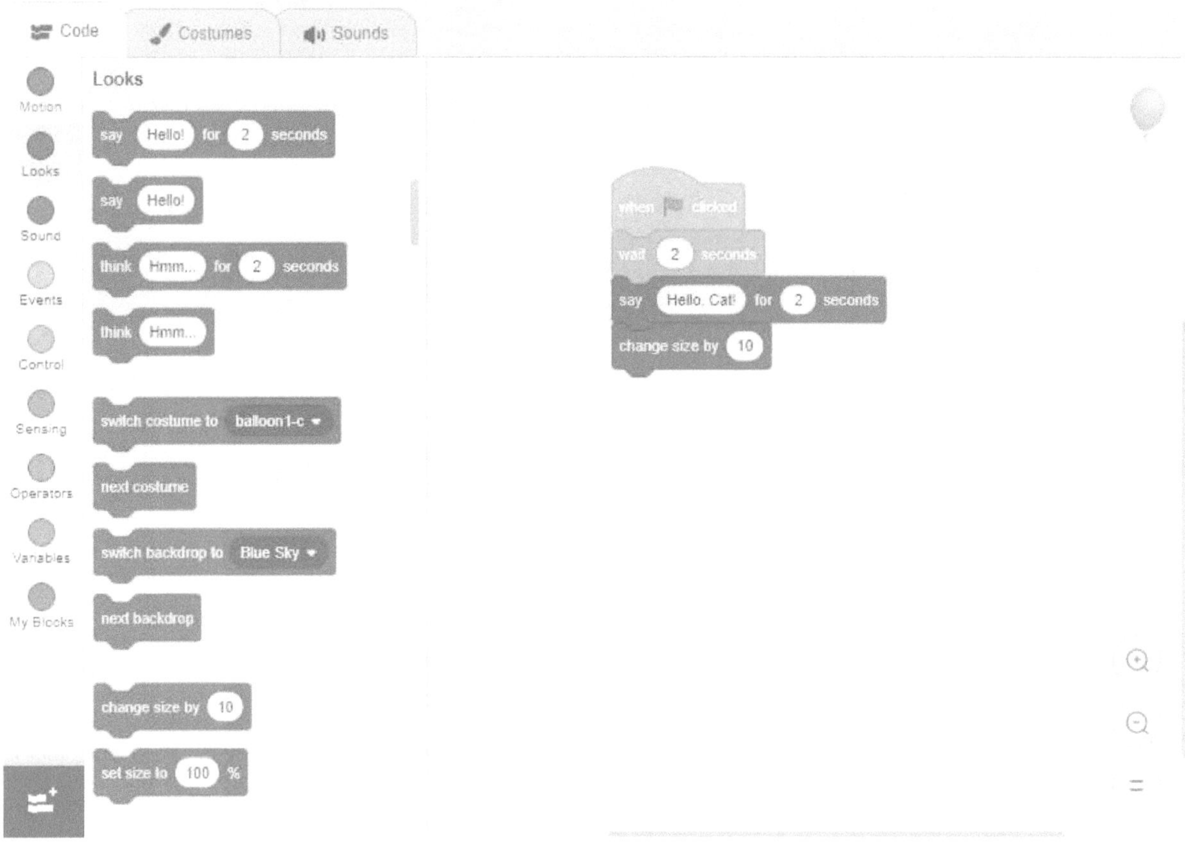

5. Test Your Project

Click the Green Flag at the top of the Stage.

Watch as the cat and the balloon greet each other and perform their actions.

6. Customizing the Project

Changing Sprites: Click the “Paint a New Sprite” button to draw your custom character.

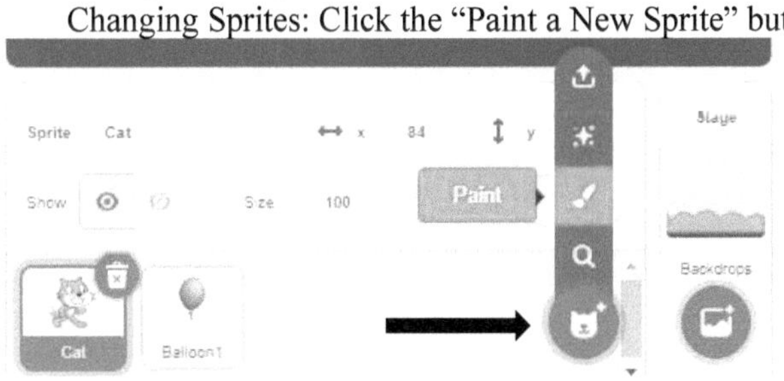

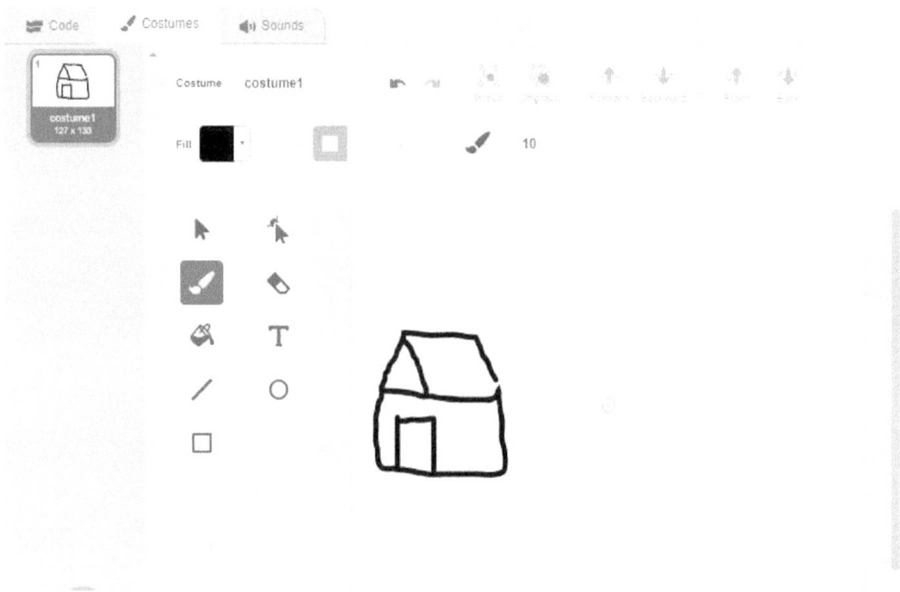

Adding Sound: Use the Sound category to add sounds or music to your sprites.

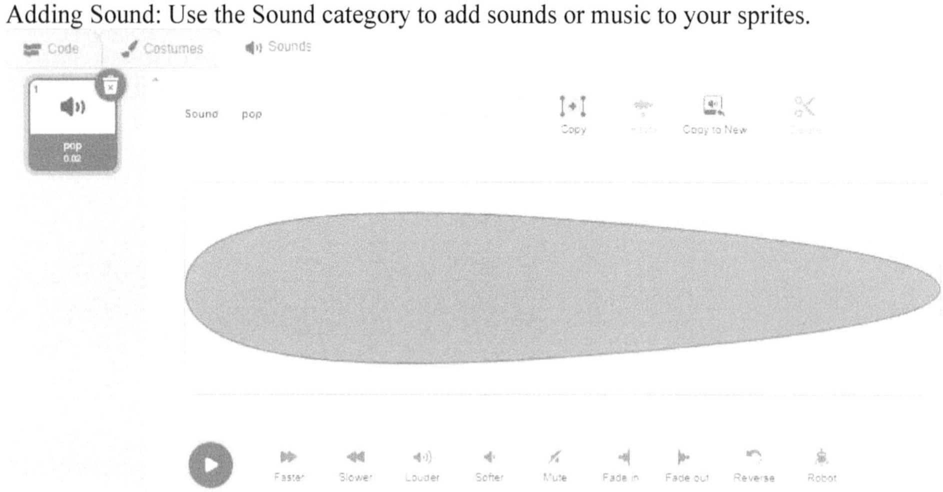

Creating Loops: Use the Forever block to repeat actions like bouncing a ball or walking continuously.

Adding Interactivity: Use the "When [space key] pressed" block to make the sprites respond to user inputs.

7. Saving

Click File > Save Now to save your work.

Project

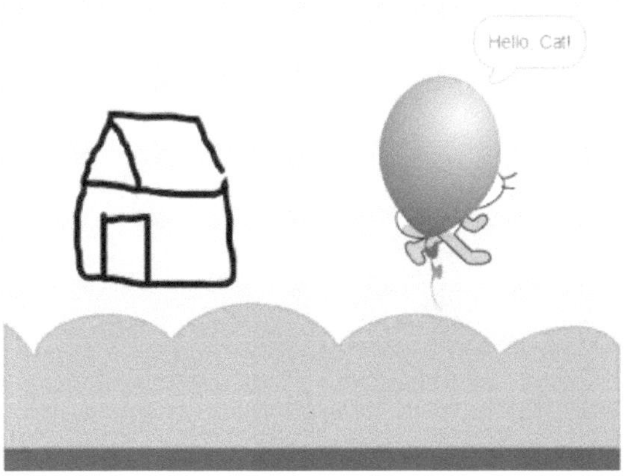

Additional Resources

CBSE Class 7 Artificial Intelligence Textbook Videos Playlist Link:
Link: https://www.youtube.com/playlist?list=PLzlh_31VWEFpxH2nttigTOi8q0OIPmYz5
QR Code:

Chapter 1 Video Playlist Link:
Link: https://www.youtube.com/playlist?list=PLzlh_31VWEFr-G3lJ7CBwGNDP4vmVyUlY
QR Code:

Chapter 2 Video Playlist Link:
Link: https://www.youtube.com/playlist?list=PLzlh_31VWEFrAsnGJGRHGgslk2ez6Mnqq
QR Code:

Chapter 3 Video Playlist Link:
Link: https://www.youtube.com/playlist?list=PLzlh_31VWEFpYufNAsTrmJlvXg4ZtAdK_
QR Code:

Chapter 4 Video Playlist Link:
Link: https://www.youtube.com/playlist?list=PLzlh_31VWEFpUlHKfNj3oPHJGPcZ-a0yf
QR Code:

Chapter 5 Video Playlist Link:
Link: https://www.youtube.com/playlist?list=PLzlh_31VWEFplZeDSfw5CT9Dn7oZw2xk-
QR Code:

Chapter 6 Video Playlist Link:
Link: https://www.youtube.com/playlist?list=PLzlh_31VWEFo49x8Jnak7Us8aRAM1S11x
QR Code:

Project Videos Playlist Link:
Link: https://www.youtube.com/playlist?list=PLzlh_31VWEFrCquPaLxdbcpWg-McMWPPt
QR Code:

Group Discussion Videos Playlist Link:
Link: https://www.youtube.com/playlist?list=PLzlh_31VWEFo0JIhtEc6fHV3yOS6j0RIl
QR Code:

Case Study Videos Playlist Link:
Link: https://www.youtube.com/playlist?list=PLzlh_31VWEFr_XKzLkREVhrWPL4lVL3Da
QR Code:

MCQs Playlist Link:
Link: https://www.youtube.com/playlist?list=PLzlh_31VWEFoz-udToZYG4X1xxSh2nJjp
QR Code:

Fill in the blanks Playlist Link:
Link: https://www.youtube.com/playlist?list=PLzlh_31VWEFrg0hT4aGlpB33npGDqD0d7
QR Code:

True or False Playlist Link:
Link: https://www.youtube.com/playlist?list=PLzlh_31VWEFq7pP31ioN0aU9Kg-oZmZtb
QR Code: